# Preface

In today's data-driven world, the ability to analyze and interpret data is essential. R, a powerful and versatile programming language, has become a leading tool for data analysis, statistics, and visualization. This book is designed to be a comprehensive guide to R programming, suitable for both beginners and experienced users. We start with the basics of R, including installation and familiarization with RStudio. From there, we cover fundamental concepts such as data types, structures, and basic operations, progressing to advanced topics like data manipulation, statistical analysis, and visualization. The book also introduces popular R packages that enhance its capabilities. Each chapter includes practical exercises and real-world examples to reinforce your learning and provide hands-on experience. By working through these exercises, you will gain a deeper understanding of R and the confidence to apply your skills to real-world problems.

Whether you are new to programming or an experienced coder looking to add R to your skillset, this book will serve as a valuable resource. By the end, you will be proficient in R programming and inspired to explore its vast possibilities. To reinforce your learning and ensure mastery of the concepts, each chapter includes:

**1. Exercises**: Thought-provoking exercises designed to test your understanding and reinforce key concepts.

**2. Activities**: Hands-on activities to apply what you've learned in real-world scenarios, fostering critical thinking and problem-solving skills.

**3. Projects**: Engaging projects that challenge you to tackle R Programming problems from start to finish, integrating multiple concepts and techniques.

**4. Test Papers**: Comprehensive test papers to assess your knowledge and track your progress throughout the course.

**5. Online Exams for Practice Questions**: Access to online exams containing additional practice questions, allowing you to reinforce your learning at your own pace.

**6. Viva Questions**: Viva questions to prepare you for oral examinations, helping you articulate your understanding of the subject with confidence.

By actively engaging with the material presented in this book, you will develop a solid understanding of R Programming principles and acquire practical skills that are highly sought after in today's job market.

Whether you aspire to pursue a career in R Programming, enhance your analytical skills, or simply satisfy your curiosity about the world of data, this book will serve as your comprehensive guide and companion on your journey.

Table of Contents

**Preface** .......... 1
**Chapter 1: Introduction to R Programming** .......... 3
**Chapter 2: Operators in R** .......... 21
**Chapter 3: Control Statement, Loops and Functions** .......... 31
**Chapter 4: Vectors** .......... 44
**Chapter 5: Lists** .......... 54
**Chapter 6: Matrix** .......... 67
**Chapter 7:Strings** .......... 83
**Chapter 8: Arrays** .......... 93
**Chapter 9: Factors** .......... 102
**Chapter 10: Data frames** .......... 111
**Chapter 11: Data frames** .......... 123
**Chapter 12: Data Interfaces** .......... 152

# Chapter 1: Introduction to R Programming

**In this chapter you will learn about:**
- Overview and Evolution of R
- Features of R
- Advantages and Disadvantages of R
- Installation of R and R Studio
- Installation and Loading of R Packages
- R-Basic Syntax
- Data Types and Objects
- Variables
- Constants

R is a **versatile programming language designed for statistical computing, data analysis, and graphical representation**. Developed in the **early 1990s by Ross Ihaka and Robert Gentleman** at the **University of Auckland, New Zealand.** R is essential in data science and statistics due to its extensive statistical capabilities, advanced data manipulation tools, and high-quality graphics. Maintained by the R Development Core Team, R is n implementation of the S programming language with lexical scoping semantics.

It supports modular programming and integration with C, C++, .Net, Python, and FORTRAN for enhanced efficiency. As an open-source language, R benefits from a large, active community that continuously improves its functionality through a vast ecosystem of packages. Today, R is a vital tool for researchers, data analysts, statisticians, and marketers to retrieve, clean, analyze, visualize, and present data.

## 1.1 Evolution of R

**Origins and Early Development**
- **1993**: Development of R begins by Ross Ihaka and Robert Gentleman at the University of Auckland, New Zealand.
- **1995**: First version of R released, designed to be user-friendly and functional for statistical computing.

**Establishment of CRAN**
- **1997**: Comprehensive R Archive Network (CRAN) established, providing a central repository for R packages and source code.

**Growth and Widespread Adoption**
- **2000s**: Gained traction in academia and research due to its flexibility and powerful data analysis capabilities.

**Industry Adoption**
- **Late 2000s to Early 2010s**: Significant uptake in industry for advanced data analytics, driving decision-making processes.

**Introduction of RStudio**
- **2011**: Release of RStudio, an integrated development environment (IDE) that simplifies writing, debugging, and managing R scripts, enhancing accessibility.

**Modern Developments**
- Continuous updates and development of new packages keep R at the forefront of data analysis and statistical computing, supported by a vibrant community.

### 1.2 Features of R

- Well-developed programming language with conditionals, loops, and user-defined functions.
- Robust facilities for data handling and storage.
- Operators for calculations on arrays, lists, vectors, and matrices.
- Comprehensive tools for data analysis.
- Graphical capabilities for data visualization and display.
- Intuitive and easy-to-learn syntax, accessible for beginners.
- Easy import and export of data in various formats like CSV and Excel.
- Functions for data cleaning, filtering, and transformation.
- Built-in functions for basic statistical analysis and data manipulation.
- Plotting functions for creating basic graphs and charts.
- User-friendly interface with RStudio.
- Tools like RMarkdown for combining code, results, and narrative text.

### 1.3 Advantages and Disadvantages

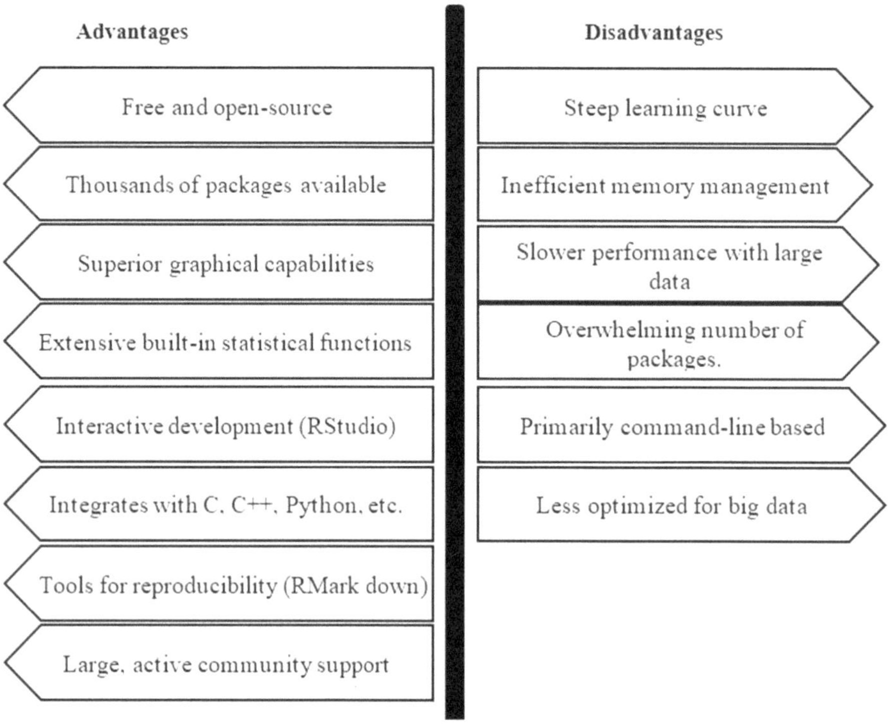


### 1.4 Installation Guide

#### 1.4.1 Installing R

**Step 1: Visit the CRAN Website**
Open your **web browser** and go to the **CRAN** (Comprehensive R Archive Network) website: **https://cran.r-project.org/.**

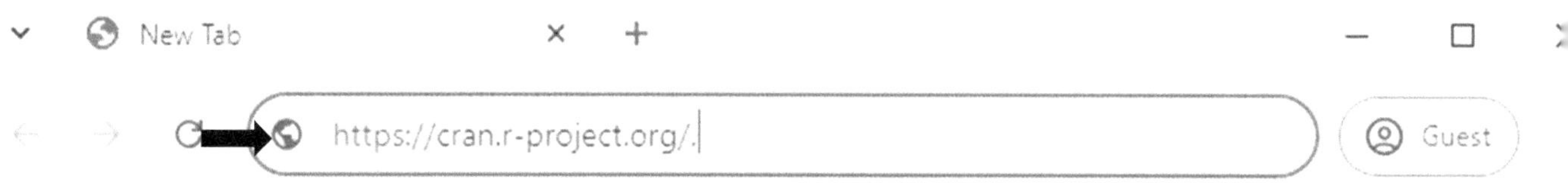


**Step 2: Choose Your Operating System**
On the CRAN homepage, you will see options for different operating systems:

- **Windows**: Click on "Download R for Windows."
- **macOS**: Click on "Download R for (Mac) OS X."
- **Linux**: Click on the link corresponding to your Linux distribution (e.g., Debian, Ubuntu, Redhat, CentOS, etc.).

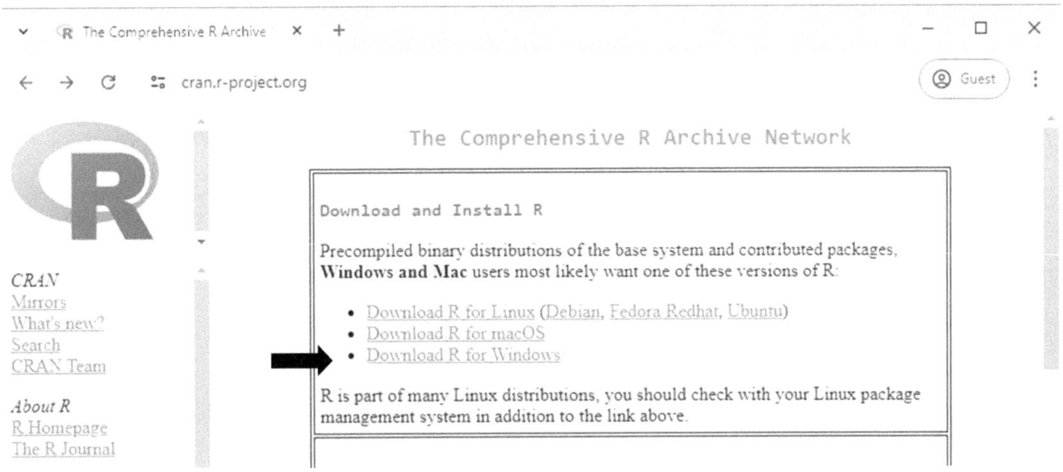


In this case we choose "**Download R for Windows**"

**Step 3: Download R Installer**
Depending on your operating system, follow these steps:

- Windows:
- Click on "**base**" to download the basic R version.

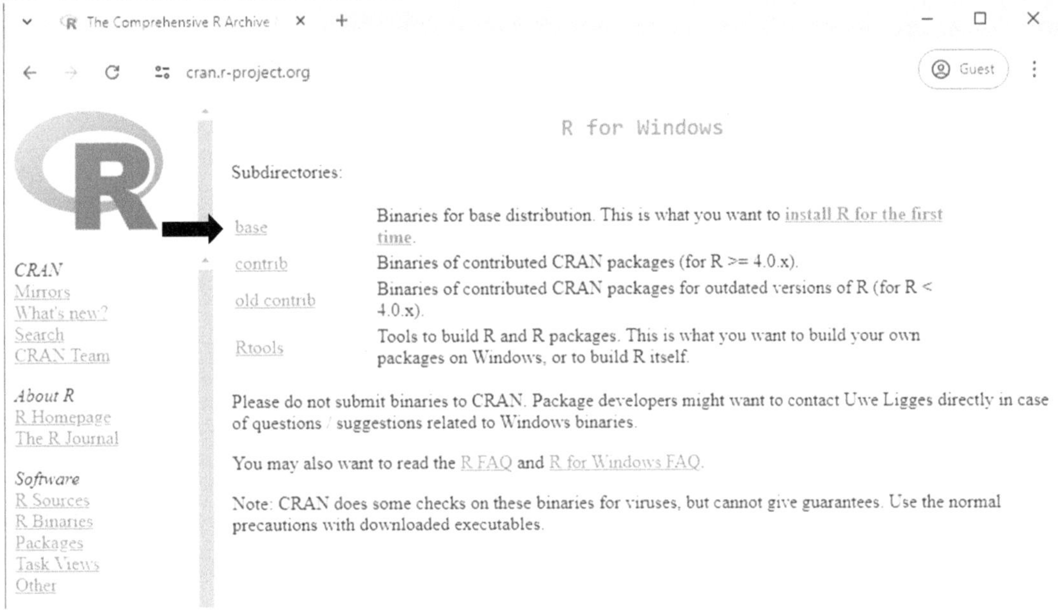


- Click on the **link** to **download the latest version** of R for Windows.

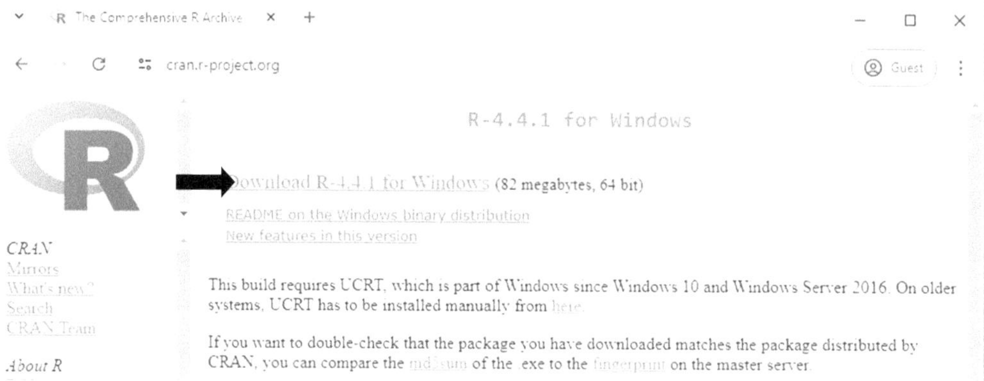


- Save the **.exe** file to your computer.

- macOS:
- Click on the link to download the latest **.pkg** file.
- Save the **.pkg** file to your computer.

- Linux:
- Follow the instructions specific to your Linux distribution provided on the CRAN page. This typically involves adding a CRAN repository and using your package manager to install R.

**Step 4: Run the Installer**

Once the download is complete, run the installer:
- Windows:
- Double-click the downloaded **.exe** file.
- Select the language then click on Next.

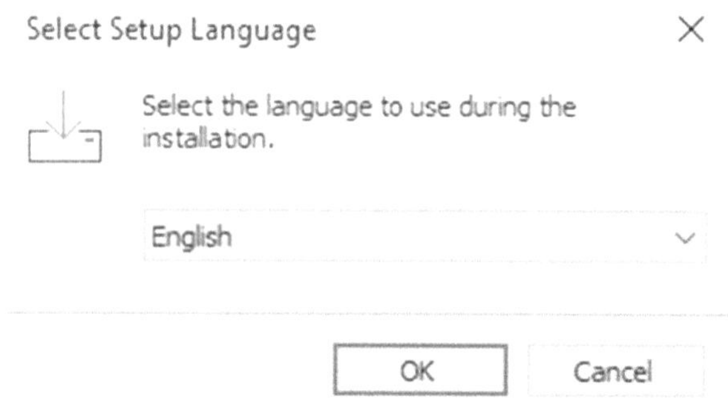


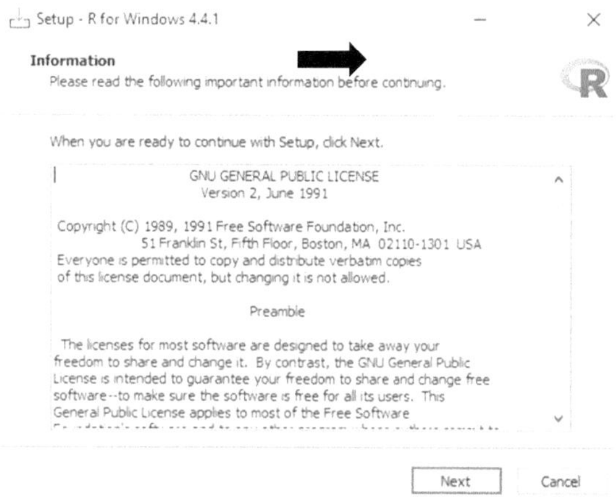


- Select the **path** where we want to download the R and proceed to Next.

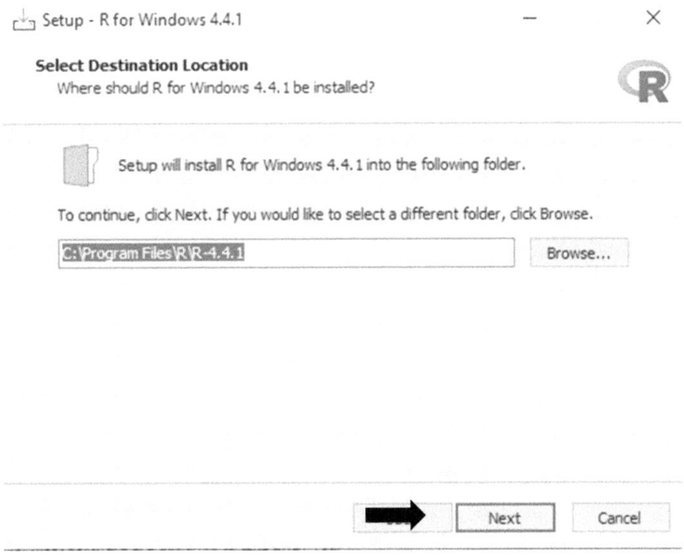


- Select all components which we want to install, and then we will proceed to **Next.**

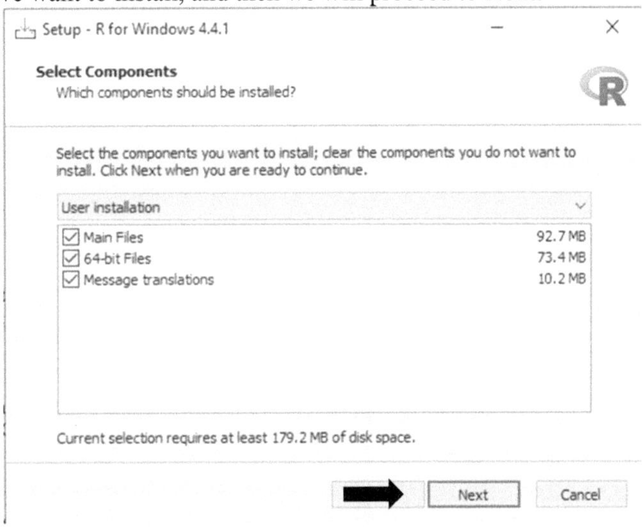


- In the next step, we have to select either customized startup or accept the default, and then we proceed to **Next.**

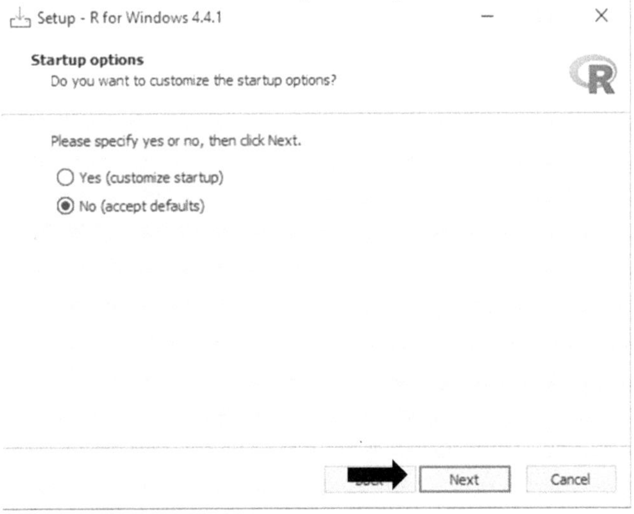

- When we proceed to next, our installation of R in our system will get started:
- In the last, we will click on finish to successfully install R in our system.

- **macOS:** Double-click the downloaded .pkg file and follow the installation instructions.
- **inux**: Follow the installation commands provided for your distribution.

### 1.2.2 Installing RStudio

**Step 1: Visit the RStudio Official Website** or got the **link** https://www.rstudio.com/products/rstudio/download.

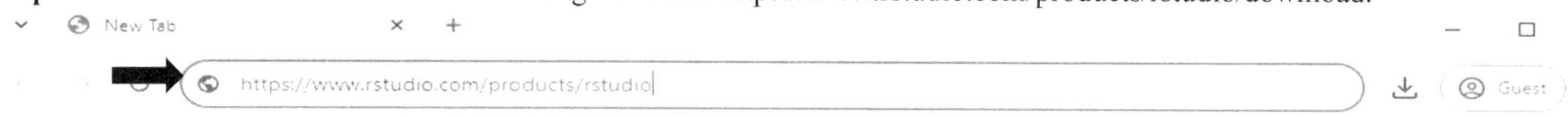


**Step 2: Click** on Download Rstudio under Rstudio Desktop.

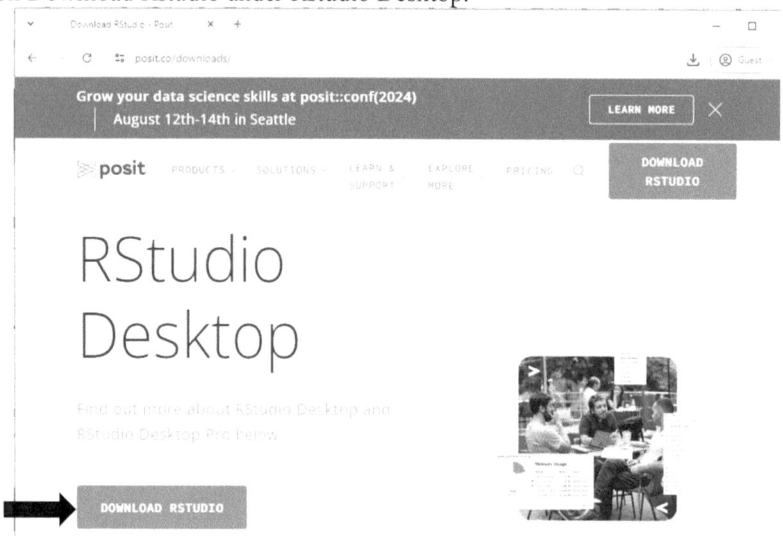


**Step 3: Click** on Download Rstudio For Desktop.

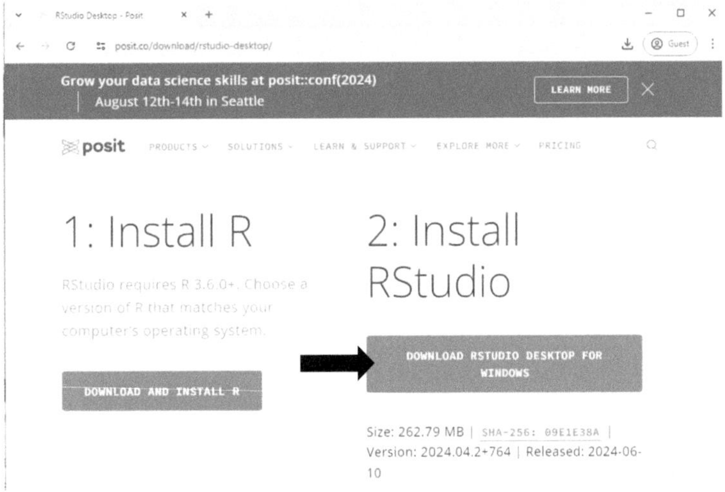


**Step 4: Run** Rstudio setup and click on **Next** then choose the file path and again click on **Next.**

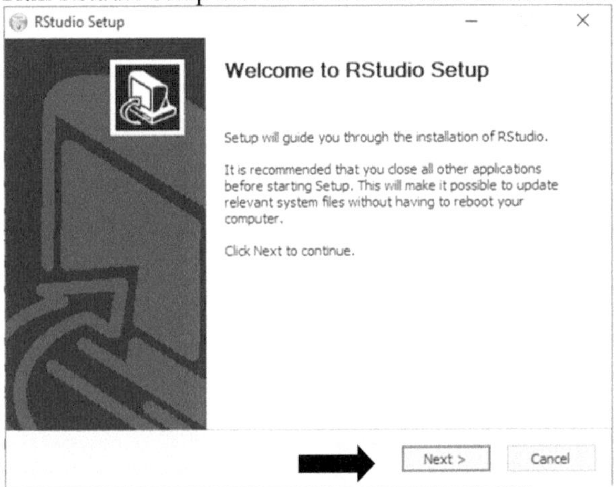


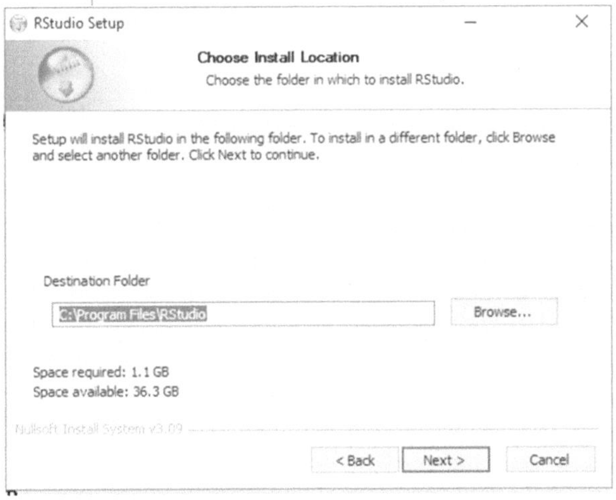


**Step 5**: Select **Rstudio** and click on **Install.**

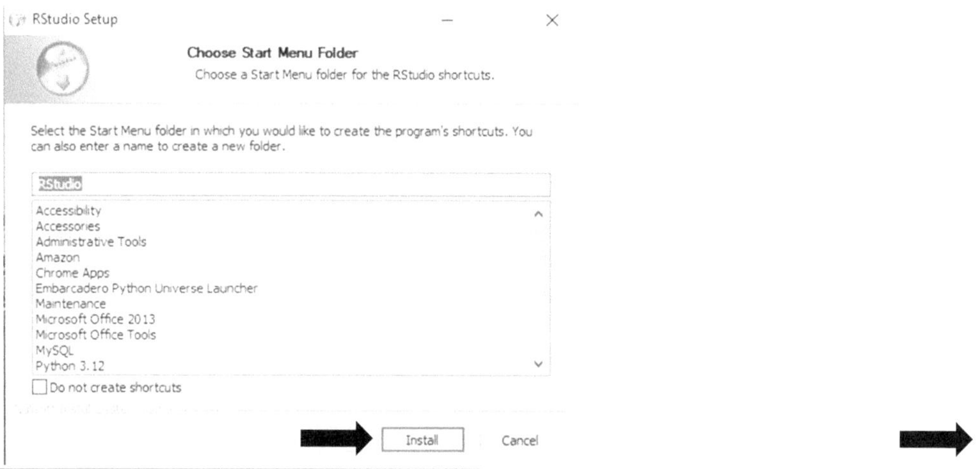

**Step 6:** Rstudio is **ready** to work.

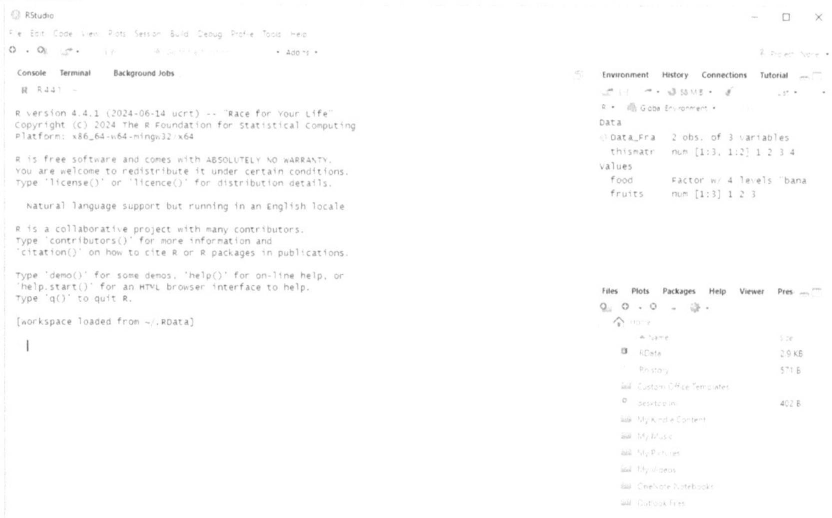


**1.5 Installation and Loading of R Packages**

**Step 1: Install a Package**

To install a package in R, you use the install.packages() function. This function downloads the package from CRAN and installs it on your system.

**- Open R or RStudio:** Ensure that you have R or RStudio open.
- Use the install.packages() function:

**Syntax:**

```
install.packages("package_name")
```

Replace **"package_name"** with the name of the package you want to install. For example, to install the **ggplot2** package, you would use:

```
install.packages("ggplot2")
```

**Step 2: Load a Package**

After installing a package, you need to load it into your R session using the **library()** function.

**- Use the library() function**:

```
library("package_name")
```

- Replace package_name with the name of the package you want to load. For example, to load the ggplot2 package, you would use:

```
library(ggplot2)
```

**Additional**

**- Installing Multiple Packages:** You can install multiple packages at once by passing a vector of package names to **install.packages()**.

```
install.packages(c("ggplot2", "dplyr", "tidyr"))
```

**- Updating Packages**: To update all installed packages, use the **update.packages()** function.

```
update.packages()
```

**- Checking Installed Packages**: To see a list of all installed packages, use the `installed.packages()` function.

```
installed.packages()
```

By following these steps, you can easily install and load packages in R, extending its functionality and making your data analysis tasks more efficient and effective.

**1.6 R-Basic Syntax**

The "Hello, World!" program is a simple way to demonstrate the basic syntax for writing and executing a program in R. Here is how you can create and run a basic "Hello, World!" program in R.

```
> print("Hello World!")
[1] "Hello World!"
```

**1.7 Data Types in R**

R supports a variety of data types that are crucial for data analysis and statistical computations. Here are the primary data types in R:

1. Numeric

Numeric data types are used to represent real numbers, which include integers, floating-point numbers, and double-precision numbers. By default, numbers in R are stored as double-precision floating-point numbers.

```
> num<-6.5
> print(num)
[1] 6.5
> print(class(num))
[1] "numeric"
> print(typeof(num))
[1] "double"
```

2. Integer

Integers are whole numbers. To explicitly define an integer in R, use the "**L**" suffix.

```
> num<-42L
> print(num)
[1] 42
> print(class(num))
[1] "integer"
> print(typeof(num))
[1] "integer"
```

3. Complex

Complex numbers have both real and imaginary parts. In R, complex numbers are represented using the **"i"** suffix for the imaginary part.

```
> num<-2+3i
> print(num)
[1] 2+3i
> print(class(num))
[1] "complex"
> print(typeof(num))
[1] "complex"
```

4. Logical

Logical data types represent Boolean values, **TRUE** or **FALSE**. Logical values are often used in conditional statements and logical operations.

```
> num<-TRUE
> print(num)
[1] TRUE
> print(class(num))
[1] "logical"
> print(typeof(num))
[1] "logical"
```

5. Character

Character data types are used to store text or string data. Strings in R are enclosed in double quotes.

```
> char1<-"Hello Students!"
> print(char1)
[1] "Hello Students!"
> print(class(char1))
[1] "character"
> print(typeof(char1))
[1] "character"
```

**1.8 Variables in R**

Variables in R are used to **store data values**. They are containers that hold information which can be referenced and manipulated in the program.

**Creating Variables**
Variables are created using the **assignment operator <- or** =. The preferred assignment operator in R is <-.because the = operator can be forbidden in some context in R.

x <- 10 (Using the preferred assignment operator)

y = 5 (Using the equal sign assignment operator)

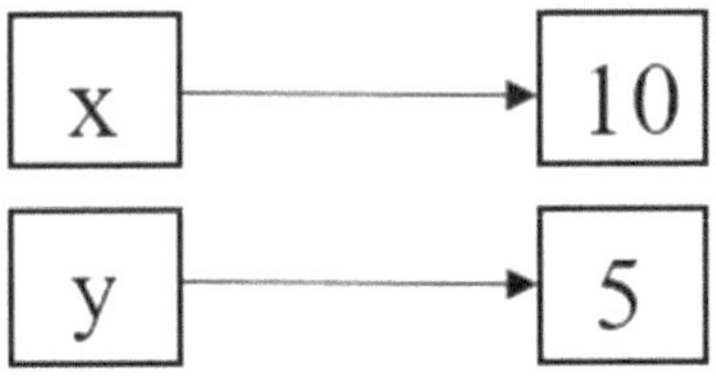


**Variable NamingRules**
- Names can contain letters, numbers, dots, and underscores.
- Names must start with a letter or a dot (not followed by a number).
- Names are case-sensitive.

**Invalid Variables:**
- Cannot start with a number.
- Cannot contain spaces or special characters like -, !, etc.
- Cannot use reserved words (e.g., TRUE, NULL, for).

| Name of Variable | Validity | Reason for Validity or Invalidity |
|---|---|---|
| **_var_name** | Invalid | Variable names cannot start with an underscore (_). |
| **var_name, var.name** | Valid | Variables can start with a letter or a dot (not followed by a number). |
| **var_name%** | Invalid | Special characters are not allowed in variable names except dot and underscore. |
| **2var_name** | Invalid | Variable names cannot start with a numeric digit. |
| **.2var_name** | Invalid | A variable name cannot start with a dot followed by a digit. |
| **var_name2** | Valid | The variable contains letters, numbers, and underscores, and starts with a letter. |
| **.var_name** | Valid | Variables can start with a dot, provided it is not followed by a number. |
| **var name** | Invalid | Variable names cannot contain spaces. |

## 1.9 Comments
Comments in R are annotations in the code that are not executed. They are used to explain and document the code, making it easier for others (or yourself) to understand the logic and purpose behind specific code segments. Comments can be particularly helpful for debugging, code maintenance, and collaboration.

**Types of Comments**
1. Single-Line Comments

Single-line comments begin with the # symbol and extend to the end of the line. These are used for short explanations or annotations.

```
> # This is a single-line comment
> num<-15 #This comment explains the variable num
```

2. Multi-Line Comments

R does not support multi-line comments directly. However, you can use multiple single-line comments to achieve the same effect.

```
> # This is a multi-line comment
> # Each line starts with the # symbol
> # to continue the comment across multiple lines.
> num<-20
> print(num)
[1] 20
```

**Summary**

- **R Programming:** Developed in the 1990s by Ross Ihaka and Robert Gentleman for statistical computing, data analysis, and graphics; open-source with strong community support.
- Evolution:
- **1993:** Development begins.
- **1995:** First version released.
- **1997:** CRAN established.
- **2011:** RStudio released.
- **Features:** Advanced statistical and graphical capabilities, robust data handling, intuitive syntax, extensive package ecosystem.
- **Advantages:** Strong community support, cross-platform compatibility, wide range of packages.
- **Disadvantages:** Steep learning curve, performance issues with large datasets.
- **Installation:** Download R from CRAN and run the installer; download RStudio from its website and install; install packages using install.packages() and load with library().

**Glossary**

- **CRAN:** Central repository for R packages and source code.
- **IDE**: Integrated Development Environment; software for comprehensive programming facilities.
- **Lexical Scoping:** Rule in R for resolving variable names in nested functions.
- **RStudio:** IDE for R, enhancing usability and accessibility.
- **Packages:** Collections of R functions, data, and compiled code.
- **Syntax:** Rules defining R program construction.
- **Numeric Data Type:** Represents real numbers, including integers and floating-point numbers.
- **Logical Data Type:** Boolean values (TRUE or FALSE).
- **Character Data Type:** Represents text strings.
- **Comments:** Annotations in the code for documentation and explanation, not executed.

## Exercises

**Exercise 1 – Multiple Choice Questions**

1. Who developed R programming?
   a) James Gosling    b) Guido van Rossum
   c) Ross Ihaka and Robert Gentleman    d) Bjarne Stroustrup
2. What does CRAN stand for?
   a) Comprehensive R Archive Network    b) Central R Archive Node
   c) Complete R Application Network    d) Comprehensive R Application Node
3. Which year was the first version of R released?
   a) 1993    b) 1995    c) 1997    d) 2011
4. What is a key feature of R?
   a) Limited data handling    b) Advanced statistical capabilities
   c) Poor graphical capabilities    d) Proprietary software
5. Which operator is used for assignment in R?
   a) =    b) <-    c) :=    d) =>

**Exercise 2 – True/False**

1. R was developed in the early 1990s.    (    )

2. CRAN stands for Central R Archive Network. ( )
3. RStudio is an IDE for Python. ( )
4. Logical data types in R can be TRUE or FALSE. ( )
5. R is a closed-source programming language. ( )

**Exercise 3 – Fill in the blanks**
1. R is a _______ programming language.
2. The first version of R was released in _______.
3. CRAN provides a central repository for R _______ and source code.
4. RStudio was released in _______.
5. R supports _______ programming and integration with C, C++, .Net, Python, and FORTRAN.

**Exercise 4- Fill in the blanks with two options**
1. R was developed by _______ and _______.
2. The main repository for R packages is _______ which stands for _______.
3. R was designed for _______ and _______.
4. The IDE for R released in 2011 is _______ which enhances _______.
5. R provides advanced _______ and _______ capabilities.

**Exercise 5- Rearrange the sentence**
1. Developed, R, 1990s, the, in, was.
2. Is, IDE, an, RStudio, for, R.
3. Stands, CRAN, Comprehensive, Archive, Network, R, for.
4. For, computing, data, R, statistical, designed, and, analysis, was.
5. Packages, repository, a, CRAN, central, provides, for.

**Exercise 6- Choose the Odd One Out**
1. RStudio, CRAN, IDE, Python
2. Numeric, Integer, Text, Complex
3. R, C++, Python, Java
4. Mean, Median, Mode, Text
5. CRAN, RStudio, GitHub, Bioconductor

**Exercise 7- Jumble words**
1. ertavseli ______________
2. sutrdoi ______________
3. tnempolved ______________
4. epmaeiltnonti ______________
5. gnimmargorg ______________

**Exercise 8- Match the case**

| | |
|---|---|
| 1. RStudio | a) Co-developer of R |
| 2. CRAN | b) IDE for R |
| 3. Numeric | c) Data type for boolean values (TRUE or FALSE) |
| 4. Ross Ihaka | d) Central repository for R packages |
| 5. Logical | e) Data type for real numbers |

**Exercise 9- Assertion – Reason**
Each question consists of two statements: an Assertion (A) and a Reason (R). Use the following codes to select the correct answer:
1. Both Assertion (A) and Reason (R) are the true and Reason (R) is a correct explanation.
2. Both Assertion (A) and Reason (R) are the true but Reason (R) is not a correct explanation.
3. Assertion (A) is true and Reason (R) is false.
4. Assertion (A) is false and Reason (R) is true.
1. **Assertion:** R is used for statistical computing.
**Reason:** R was designed for graphical representation and data analysis.

2. **Assertion:** CRAN is an IDE for R.
**Reason:** CRAN stands for Comprehensive R Archive Network.
3. **Assertion:** R is an open-source language.
**Reason:** Open-source languages are developed by a community of contributors.
4. **Assertion:** R was developed in the 1980s.
**Reason:** R was designed for statistical computing.
5. **Assertion:** Logical data types in R include TRUE or FALSE.
**Reason:** Logical data types are used for conditional statements.

**Exercise 10- Read the questions given below and find the appropriate word in the grid provided.**
1. Software for R development?
2. Repository for R packages?
1. Popular IDE for R?
2. Collections of R functions?
3. Data type for real numbers?

| R | P | A | C | K | A | G | E | S | N |
|---|---|---|---|---|---|---|---|---|---|
| S | G | U | p | V | D | E | E | O | U |
| T | O | P | C | W | R | V | P | M | M |
| U | R | L | R | D | V | I | I | O | E |
| D | L | M | A | F | F | S | D | I | R |
| I | H | F | N | S | R | N | E | M | I |
| O | U | R | Z | C | C | E | P | M | C |
| H | P | S | Q | A | A | J | R | A | T |
| V | I | V | W | D | P | E | O | R | I |
| T | Q | W | T | A | C | R | M | G | C |

**Exercise 11- Give two answers for the following.**
1. Types of Data in R ____________, ____________
2. Programming Languages Integrated with R ____________, ____________
3. R Functions for Data Visualization ____________, ____________
4. Statistical Measures in R ____________, ____________
5. R Development Tools ____________, ____________

**Exercise 12- One- word**
1. Who co-developed R?
2. What is the central repository for R packages?
3. Which IDE is popular for R?
4. What type of data does TRUE/FALSE represent?
5. Which year was RStudio released?

**Exercise 13- Small Answers**
1. What does CRAN stand for and what is its purpose?
2. Who are the developers of the R programming language?
3. What is RStudio and what role does it play in R programming?
4. What is the primary use of the R programming language?
5. How can you install a package in R?

**Exercise 14- Long Answers**
1. Describe the evolution of R from its development to the introduction of RStudio.
2. What are the primary features of R, and how do they contribute to its widespread use in data science?
3. Explain the installation process for R and RStudio.
4. Discuss the advantages and disadvantages of using R for data analysis.
5. Explain the various data types in R with their characteristics and usage.

## Answers

**Exercise 1** – 1. c) 2. a) 3. b) 4. b) 5.b)
**Exercise 2** – 1. True 2. False 3. False 4. True 5. False
**Exercise 3** – 1. Versatile 2. 1995 3. Packages 4. 2011 5. Modular
**Exercise 4** – 1. Ross Ihaka, Robert Gentleman 2. CRAN, Comprehensive R Archive Network 3. statistical computing,
data analysis 4. RStudio, usability 5. statistical, graphical
**Exercise 5** – 1. R was developed in the 1990s.
2. RStudio is an IDE for R.
3. CRAN stands for Comprehensive R Archive Network.
4. R was designed for statistical computing and data analysis.
5. CRAN provides a central repository for packages.
**Exercise 6** – 1. Python 2. Text 3. R 4. Text 5. GitHub
**Exercise 7** – 1. Versatile 2. RStudio 3. Development 4. Implementation 5. Programming
**Exercise 8** – 1. b) 2. d) 3. e) 4. a) 5. c)
**Exercise 9** – 1. a) 2. d) 3. a) 4. d) 5. a)
**Exercise 10** – 1. IDE
2. CRAN
3. RStudio
4. Packages
5. Numeric

| **R** | **P** | **A** | **C** | **K** | **A** | **G** | **E** | **S** | **N** |
|---|---|---|---|---|---|---|---|---|---|
| S | G | U | p | V | D | E | E | O | **U** |
| **T** | O | P | **C** | W | R | V | P | M | **M** |
| **U** | R | L | **R** | D | V | I | **I** | O | **E** |
| **D** | L | M | **A** | F | F | S | **D** | I | **R** |
| **I** | H | F | **N** | S | R | N | **E** | M | **I** |
| **O** | U | R | Z | C | C | E | P | M | **C** |
| H | P | S | Q | A | A | J | R | A | T |
| V | I | V | W | D | P | E | O | R | I |
| T | Q | W | T | A | C | R | M | G | C |

**Exercise 11** – 1. Numeric, Character 2. C++, Python 3. ggplot2, plot() 4. Mean, Median 5. RStudio, CRAN
**Exercise 12** – 1. Ross 2. CRAN 3. RStudio 4. Logical 5. 2011

## Online Resources

### Online Practice Paper

**MCQ Form**
**Link**
https://forms.gle/nSSbChkXKKfhsNze8
**QR Code**

**True or False**
**Link**
https://forms.gle/bpZeF1zTQ85pBrjP8
QR Code

**Fill in the blank**
**Link** https://forms.gle/AcjNtxkAvKD1XH25A
**QR Code**

**Fill in the blank with two options**
**Link** https://forms.gle/cCEjeD6LJ9qX3Fgb8
**QR Code**

### Project Video Link

**Link**
https://www.youtube.com/playlist?list=PLzlh_31VWEFoXTJqrHt_nW5s247CwygsR
**QR Code**

## YouTube Video Playlist Link

**Link**
https://www.youtube.com/playlist?list=PLzlh_31VWEFoXTJqrHt_nW5s247CwygsR
**QR Code**

**Test Paper**
**Chapter-1**
**Introduction to R Programming**

**Time Duration: 40 Minutes** **Maximum Marks: 25**

**General Instructions:**

1. The question paper consists of 12 questions and is divided into four sections, A, B, C and D.
2. All questions are compulsory.
3. Section A comprises MCQs, Fill in the blanks and True or False carrying one marks each.
4. Section B comprises VSAQs(very short answers questions) carrying two marks each.
5. Section C comprises SAQs(short questions) carrying four marks each.
6. Section D comprises long questions carrying five marks each.

## SECTION-A

**I. Multiple choice questions:** **(1*2=2)**

1. Which year was the first version of R released?

   a) 1993 b) 1995
   c) 1997 d) 2011

2. What is RStudio used for?

   a) Web development b) Writing, debugging, and managing R scripts
   c) Data storage d) Game development

**II. Fill in the blanks:** **(1*2=2)**

1. R is a versatile programming language designed for __________ computing, data analysis, and graphical representation.
2. The first version of R was released in the year __________.

**III. True or False: (1*2=2)**

1. CRAN is the central repository for R packages and source code.
2. RStudio was released in the year 1997.

## SECTION-B

**IV. Very Short answers type questions-I** **(2*3=6)**

1. Who developed R programming language?
2. What is CRAN?
3. What is the primary use of R?

## SECTION-C

**V. Short answers type questions-II** **(4*2=8)**

1. What are the advantages of using R?
2. Describe the process to install a package in R.

## SECTION-D

**VI. Long answers type questions** **(5*1=5)**

1. Discuss the evolution and key features of R programming language.

# Chapter 2: Operators in R

**In this chapter you will learn about:**

- Introduction to Operators
- Arithmetic Operators
- Relational Operators
- Logical Operators
- Assignment Operators
- Miscellaneous Operators

## 2.1 Introduction to Operators in R

Operators in R are symbols that perform operations on variables and values. These operations are crucial for data manipulation, analysis, and computation in R programming. Understanding the different types of operators and their functions is fundamental to writing effective and efficient R code.

### Types of Operators in R

- Arithmetic Operators
- Relational Operators
- Logical Operators
- Assignment Operators
- Miscellaneous Operator

<table>
<tr><td>+</td><td>-</td><td>*</td><td>/</td><td>^</td><td>%%</td><td>%/%</td></tr>
<tr><td>></td><td><</td><td>>=</td><td><=</td><td>==</td><td>!=</td><td></td></tr>
<tr><td>!</td><td>&</td><td>&&</td><td>|</td><td>||</td><td></td><td></td></tr>
<tr><td>=</td><td><-</td><td>-></td><td><<-</td><td>->></td><td></td><td></td></tr>
<tr><td>:</td><td>%in%</td><td>%*%</td><td></td><td></td><td></td><td></td></tr>
</table>

## 2.2 Arithmetic Operators

Arithmetic operators in R are used for basic mathematical operations. They allow you to perform calculations on numerical data, which are fundamental to data analysis and programming in R. Here are the primary arithmetic operators:

Take the two numbers and perform below operations:

```
num1 <- 5
num2 <- 10
```

Assign values 5 and 10 to the variable num1 and num2

**2.2.1 Addition (+):** Adds two numbers.
- Syntax : x + y
- Example :

```
sum <- num1 + num2      ← Add two numbers
print(sum)              ← Print the result using print() function
15                      ← Output
```

**2.2.3 Subtraction (-):** Subtracts one number from another.
- Syntax : x - y
- Example :

```
diff <- num1 - num2     ← Difference of two numbers
print(diff)
-5                      ← Output
```

**2.2.3 Multiplication (*) :** Multiplies two numbers.
- Syntax : x * y
- Example :

```
multiply <- num1 * num2     ← Multiplication of two numbers
print(multiply)
50                          ← Output
```

**2.2.4 Division (/) :** Divides one number by another.
- Syntax : x / y
- Example :

```
division <- num1 / num2     ← Division of two numbers
print(division)
0.5
```

**2.2.5 Exponentiation (^ or **) :** Raises one number to the power of another
- Syntax : x ^ y or x ** y
- Example :

```
exponent <- num1 ^ num2
print(exponent)
9765625
```

Or num1 ** num2 can also use

**2.2.6 Modulus ( %% ) :** Returns the remainder of a division
- Syntax : x %% y
- Example :

```
remainder <- num1 %% num2
print(remainder)
5
```

Remainder of two numbers

**2.2.7 Integer Division ( %/%) :** Returns the integer part of a division of one number by another.
- Syntax : x %/% y
- Example :

```
intdivision <- num1 %/% num2
print(intdivision)
0
```

Integer Division of two numbers

**Vectorized Operations**

One of the powerful features of R is its ability to perform arithmetic operations on entire vectors, applying the operation element-wise.

**Example:**

```
v1 <- c(1,2)
v2 <- c(3,4)

#Addition
add <- v1 + v2
print(add)
4 6 #output

#Subtraction
sub <- v1 – v2
print(sub)
-2 -2 #output

#Multiplication
multiply <- v1 * v2
print(multiply)
3 8 #output

#Division
div <- v1 / v2
print(div)
0.3333333 0.5000000 #output
```

```
v1 <- c(1,2)
v2 <- c(3,4)

#Exponentiation
exp <- v1 ^ v2
print(exp)
1 16 #output

#Modulus
modulus <- v1 %% v2
print(modulus)
1 2 #output

#Integer Division
Int_div <- v1 %/% v2
print(int_div)
0 0 #output
```

### 2.3 Logical Operators

Logical operators in R are used to perform logical operations on values, combining multiple conditions or inverting them. They are essential for decision-making and control flow in programming. Here are the main logical operators:

#### 2.3.1 Logical AND Operator

The logical AND operator in R is used to combine multiple conditions and evaluate whether both (or all) conditions are true. R provides two types of AND operators: & and &&.

**1. Single Element AND (&&):** This operator is used to combine two conditions and checks only the first element of each logical vector. It is primarily used in control flow statements such as if statements where you only need to evaluate the first element.

- **Syntax**: `condition1 && condition2`
- **Example:**

```
x <-TRUE
y <- FALSE
result <- x && y
print(result)
FALSE
```

Condition

Output

**2. Vectorized AND (&):** This operator is used to perform element-wise logical AND operations on vectors. It evaluates each pair of elements in the two vectors.

- **Syntax:** vector1 & vector2
- Example:

```
v1 <- c(TRUE, FALSE, TRUE)
v2 <- c(TRUE, TRUE, FALSE)
result <- v1 & v2
print(result)
TRUE FALSE FALSE
```

Condition

Output

#### 2.3.2 Logical OR Operator in R

The logical OR operator in R is used to combine multiple conditions and evaluate whether at least one of the conditions is true. Similar to the AND operator, R provides two types of OR operators: | and ||.

**1. Single Element OR (||):** This operator is used to combine two conditions and checks only the first element of each logical vector. It is primarily used in control flow statements such as if statements where you only need to evaluate the first element.

- **Syntax:** condition1 || condition2
- Example:

```
x <- TRUE
y <- FALSE
result <- x & y
print (result)
TRUE
```

Condition

Output

**2. Vectorized OR (|):** This operator is used to perform element-wise logical OR operations on vectors. It evaluates each pair of elements in the two vectors.

- **Syntax:** vector1 | vector2
- Example:

```
v1 <- c(TRUE, FALSE, TRUE)
v2 <- c(TRUE, TRUE, FALSE)
result <- v1 & v2
print(result)
TRUE TRUE TRUE
```

Condition

Output

### 2.3.3 Logical NOT Operator in R

The logical NOT operator in R is used to invert the logical value of a condition. If the condition is TRUE, it becomes FALSE, and if the condition is FALSE, it becomes TRUE. This operator is essential for reversing logical conditions in your code, which is particularly useful in control flow and decision-making processes.

- Operator: !
- **Syntax:** !condition
- **Function:** Inverts the truth value of the condition.
- Example:

```
x <- TRUE
result <- !x
print(result)
FALSE
```

Condition

Output

- Vectorized Example:

```
v <- c(TRUE, FALSE, TRUE)
result <- !v
print(result)
FALSE TRUE FALSE
```

Condition

Output

## 2.4 Assignment Operator

Assignment operators in R are used to assign values to variables. These operators are fundamental to programming in R, as they allow you to store and manipulate data. R primarily uses left and right assignment operators, each with its specific usage.

**2.4.1 Left Assignment** (<- , = and <<-): Assigns a value to a variable from the right side of the operator.
- **Usage**: The left assignment operator <− is the most commonly used and preferred in R for clarity and consistency, though = and <<- (also be used as global variable) can also be used.
- Example:

```
x <- 5
print(x)
5

y = 5
print(y)
5

z <<- 5
print(z)
5
```

Output

**2.4.2 Right Assignment** (-> and ->>): Assigns a value to a variable from the right side of the operator.

- **Usage:** Less commonly used, but useful in certain situations for readability.
- Example:

```
5 -> x
Print(x)
5

5 ->> y
Print(y)
5
```

Output

**2.5 Relational Operator**

Relational operators in R are used to compare two values or variables. These comparisons result in logical values (TRUE or FALSE). Relational operators are essential in decision-making, control flow, and data manipulation. Here's a detailed overview of the relational operators available in R, along with examples and explanations of their usage:

**2.5.1 Equal to (==):** Checks if two values are equal.
- Syntax: x == y
- Example:

```
num1 <- 10
num2 <- 10
result <- num1 == num2
print(result)
TRUE
```

Condition

Output

**2.5.2 Not equal to (!=):** Checks if two values are not equal.
- Syntax: x != y
- Example:

```
num1 <- 10
num2 <- 5
result <- num1 != num2
print(result)
TRUE
```

Condition

Output

**2.5.3 Greater than (>):** Checks if the left value is greater than the right value.
- Syntax: x > y
- Example:

```
num1 <- 10
num2 <- 5
result <- num1 > num2
print(result)
TRUE
```

Condition

Output

**2.5.4 Less than (<):** Checks if the left value is less than the right value.
- Syntax: x < y
- Example:

```
num1 <- 10
num2 <- 5
result <- num1 ≤ num2
print(result)
FALSE
```

Condition

Output

**2.5.5 Greater than or equal to (>=):** Checks if the left value is greater than or equal to the right value.

- Syntax: x >= y
- Example:

```
num1 <- 10
num2 <- 5
result <- num1 >= num2
print(result)
TRUE
```

Condition

Output

**2.5.6 Less than or equal to (<=):** Checks if the left value is less than or equal to the right value.

- Syntax: x <= y
- Example:

```
num1 <- 10
num2 <- 5
result <- num1 <= num2
print(result)
FALSE
```

Condition

Output

### 2.6 Operator Precedence and Associativity in R

Understanding the precedence and associativity of operators in R is crucial for writing accurate and predictable code. Precedence determines the order in which operations are performed, while associativity determines the order in which operations of the same precedence are executed.

**2.6.1 Operator Precedence:** Understanding the precedence and associativity of operators in R is essential for writing accurate and predictable code. Precedence determines the order in which operations are performed, while associativity determines the order in which operations of the same precedence are executed. Below is a table summarizing the operator precedence and associativity in R:

| Precedence Level | Operators | Description | Associativity |
|---|---|---|---|
| 1 | () | Parentheses | - |
| 2 | Function Calls | Calling functions | Left-to-right |
| 3 | ^ | Exponentiation | Right-to-left |
| 4 | +, -, ! | Unary plus, minus, and NOT | Right-to-left |
| 5 | *, /, %/%, %% | Multiplication, Division, Integer Division, Modulus | Left-to-right |
| 6 | +, - | Addition, Subtraction | Left-to-right |
| 7 | : | Sequence generation | Left-to-right |
| 8 | <, <=, >, >= | Relational operators | Left-to-right |
| 9 | ==, != | Equality operators | Left-to-right |
| 10 | & | Element-wise Logical AND | Left-to-right |
| 11 | && | Logical AND | Left-to-right |
| 12 | <-, =, <<-, ->, ->> | Assignment operators | Right-to-left |
| 13 | Special Operators | %*%, %in%, etc. | Left-to-right |

## 2.6.2 Operator Associativity

Associativity determines the direction of evaluation when two operators of the same precedence appear in an expression. Most operators in R are left-associative, meaning they are evaluated from left to right. The exception is the exponentiation operator (^), which is right-associative.

**Examples:**

**1. Left-Associative Operators:**

```
result <- 10 – 3 – 2 # Evaluated as (10 – 3) - 2
print(result)
5  ←———  Output
```

2. **Right-Associative Operator:**

```
result <- 2 ^ 3 ^ 2 # Evaluated as 2 ^ (3 ^ 2)
print(result)
512  ←———  Output
```

**Summary**

- **Operators**: Symbols that perform operations on data.
- **Arithmetic:** Operators: Perform basic calculations (+, -, *, /, ^, %%, %/%).
- **Logical Operators:** Combine or invert conditions (&, &&, |, ||, !).
- **Assignment Operators**: Assign values to variables (<-, =, <<-, ->, ->>).
- **Relational Operators**: Compare values, returning TRUE or FALSE (==, !=, >, <, >=, <=).

**Glossary**

- **Precedence:** The hierarchical order in which operations are performed in expressions.
- **Associativity:** Determines whether operators of the same precedence are evaluated from left to right or right to left.

## Exercise

**Exercise 1 – Multiple Choice Questions**

1. Which operator is used for exponentiation in R?
   a) + b) *
   c) ^ d) /
2. What is the result of the modulus operation 7 %% 3 in R?
   a) 1 b) 2
   c) 3 d) 4

**Exercise 2 – True/False**

1. The : operator is used for sequence generation in R.
2. The && operator is used for element-wise logical AND operations on vectors.

**Exercise 3 – Fill in the blanks**

1. The operator used to add two numbers in R is the __________ operator.
2. The == operator in R is used to check if two values are __________.

**Exercise 4 – Short questions**

1. What is the purpose of logical operators in R?
2. Explain the difference between the && and & operators in R.

**Exercise 5 – Long questions.**

1. Describe the different types of arithmetic operators in R and provide examples for each.
2. Explain the concept of operator precedence and associativity in R, and why it is important in programming. Provide examples to illustrate your explanation.

# Answers

**Exercise 1** – 1.c) 2. a)
**Exercise 2** – 1. True 2. False
**Exercise 3** – 1. + 2. Equal

**Online Resources**

**Practice Paper**
**Link** https://forms.gle/uL96rzZhwjdPU6Ly8
**QR Code**

**Project video Link**

**Link** https://www.youtube.com/playlist?list=PLzlh_31VWEFowmPaYw2tdGdroPuQKKxC8
**QR Code**

**YouTube Video Playlist Link**
**Link**
https://www.youtube.com/playlist?list=PLzlh_31VWEFowmPaYw2tdGdroPuQKKxC8
**QR Code**

**Test Paper**
**Chapter-2**
**Operators in R**

**Time Duration: 40 Minutes** **Maximum Marks: 25**

**General Instructions:**
1. The question paper consists of 12 questions and is divided into four sections, A, B, C and D.
2. All questions are compulsory.
3. Section A comprises MCQs, Fill in the blanks and True or False carrying one marks each.
4. Section B comprises VSAQs(very short answers questions) carrying two marks each.
5. Section C comprises SAQs(short questions) carrying four marks each.
6. Section D comprises long questions carrying five marks each.

## SECTION-A

**I. Multiple choice questions:** **(1*2=2)**

1. Which of the following is a relational operator in R?
   a) + b) &
   c) == d) %%
2. What does the && operator do in R?
   a) performs element-wise logical and
   b) combines conditions and checks only the first element of each logical vector
   c) performs logical or
   d) inverts the logical value of a condition

**II. Fill in the blanks:** **(1*2=2)**

1. The operator used to check if one value is greater than another in R is the __________ operator.
2. The %% operator in R returns the __________ of a division.

**III. True or False: (1*2=2)**

1. The <- operator is the most commonly used assignment operator in R.
2. The ! operator inverts the logical value of a condition.

## SECTION-B

**IV. Very Short answers type questions-I** **(2*3=6)**

1. What operator is used for integer division in R?
2. Which operator is used for logical NOT in R?
3. What is the symbol for the modulus operator in R?

## SECTION-C

**V. Short answers type questions-II** **(4*2=8)**

1. Explain the difference between | and || operators in R.
2. Describe the purpose of assignment operators in R and provide an example of both left and right assignment.

## SECTION-D

**VI. Long answers type questions** **(5*1=5)**

1. Discuss the different assignment operators in R and their usage with examples. Explain the difference between left and right assignment operators.

# Chapter 3: Control Statement, Loops and Functions

**In this chapter you will learn about:**

- Control Statements
- Conditional Statements
- Looping Statement
- Jump Statement
- Switch Statement in R
- Break Statement
- Loops in R
- For Loop
- While Loop
- Repeat Loop

**Control Statements**

Control Statements in R are essential for directing the flow of execution based on specific conditions and for repeating actions until certain criteria are met. Understanding these control statements is crucial for writing robust and efficient R code.

**Types of Control Statements in R:**

1. Conditional Statements
2. Looping Statements
3. Jump Statements

**3.1 Conditional Statements:** These statements allow you to execute code blocks based on whether certain conditions are true or false.

**3.1.1 If Statement**

The if statement in R executes code based on whether a condition is TRUE or FALSE. It's fundamental for decision-making in programming.

- **Syntax:**

```
if (condition) {
# Code to execute if condition is TRUE
}
```

- **Example:**

```
x <- 10
if(x > 5) {
  print("x is greater than 5")
}
```

**Output:** "x is greater than 5"

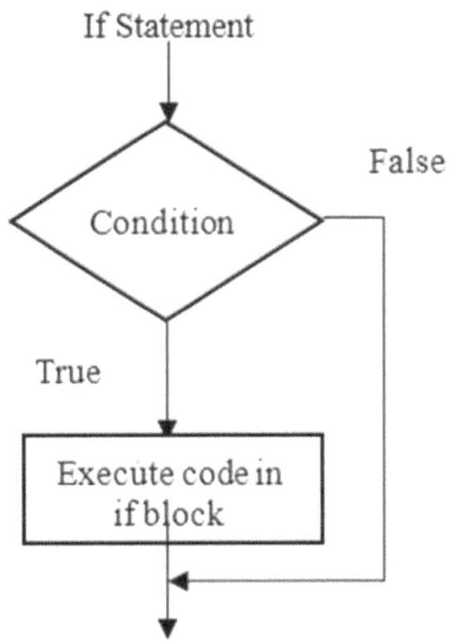


**3.1.2 If-Else Statement**

An if-else statement evaluates a condition and executes different code blocks based on the result. If the condition is true, the code within the if statement runs; if false, the code within the else statement executes.

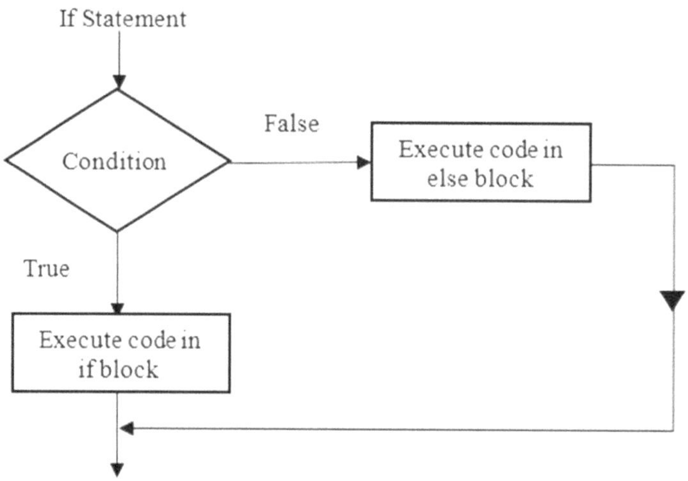


\-

\- Syntax:

```
if (condition) {
# Code to execute if condition is true
} else {
# Code to execute if condition is false
}
```

\- Example:

```
x <- 10
if (x > 15) {
  print("x is greater than 15")
} else {
  print("x is not greater than 15")
}
Output: "x is not greater than 15"
```

### 3.1.3 Else If Statement

An else if statement allows checking multiple conditions in sequence. If the first if condition is false, each subsequent else if condition is evaluated until one is true. If none are true, the else block executes

- **Syntax:**

```
if (condition1) {
 # Code to execute if condition1 is true
} else if (condition2) {
# Code to execute if condition2 is true
} else {
# Code to execute if none of the above conditions are true
}
```

- **Example:**

```
x <- 45
y <- 30
if (x > y) {
  print("x is greater than y")
} else if (x < y) {
  print("x is smaller than y")
} else {
  print("x and y are equal")
}
Output: "x is greater than y"
```

### 3.1.4 Switch Statement

The switch statement evaluates an expression and executes the corresponding block of code based on the matched value. It's useful for handling multiple conditions that depend on the value of a single variable.

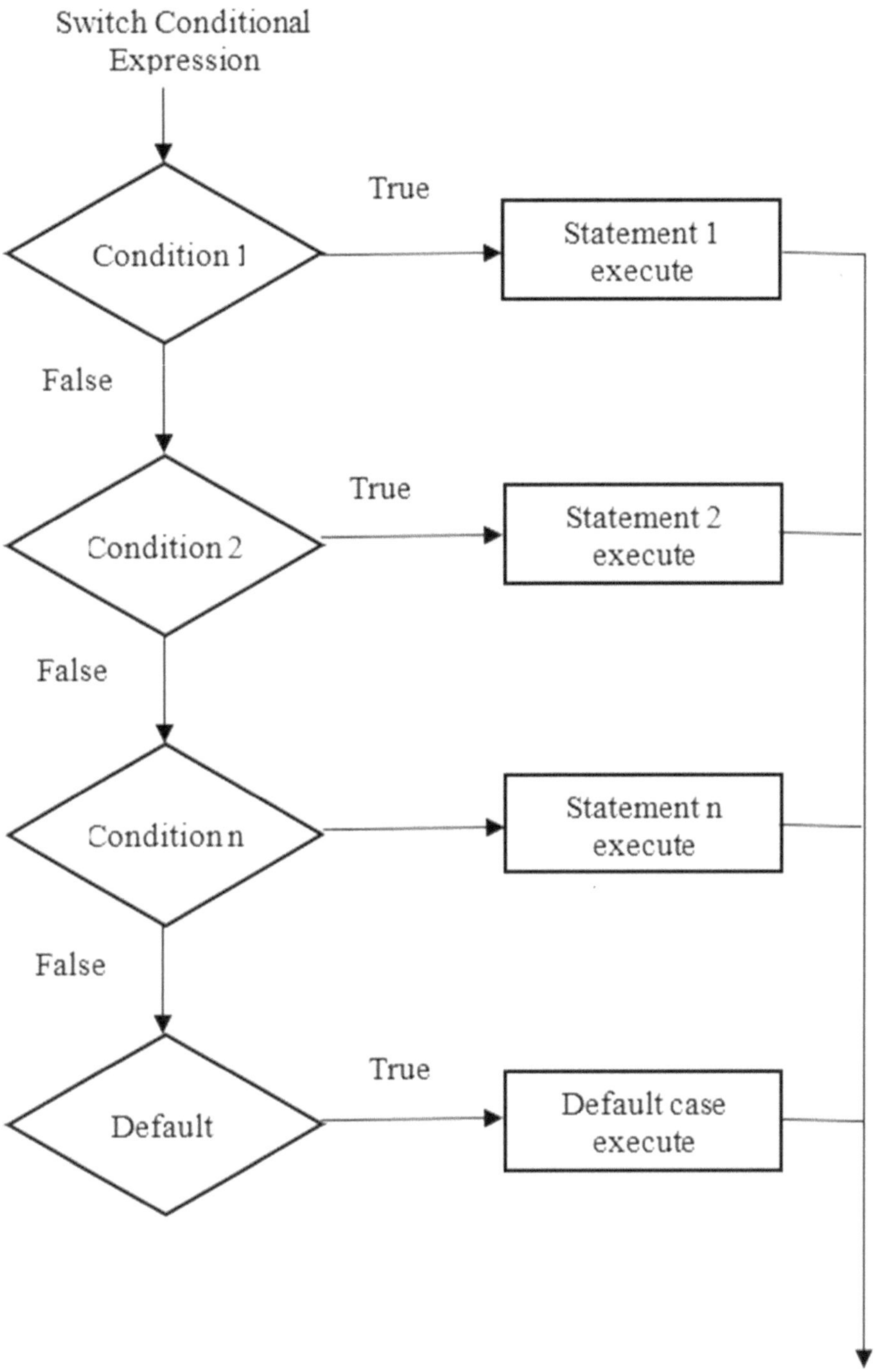
Switch Conditional
Expression
True
Condition 1
Statement 1
execute
False
True
Condition 2
Statement 2
execute
False
Condition n
Statement n
execute
False
True
Default
Default case
execute

- **Syntax:**

```
result <- switch(expression,
                 case1 = code_block1,
                 case2 = code_block2,
                 caseN = code_blockN,
                 default_code_block)
```

- **Example:**

```
day <- "Monday"
message <- switch(day,
                  "Monday"  =  "Start of the work week",
                  "Tuesday" = "Second day of the work week",
                  "Wednesday" = "Midweek",
                  "Thursday" = "Almost there",
                  "Friday" = "Last workday",
                  "Saturday" = "Weekend!",
                  "Sunday" = "Weekend!",
                  "Invalid day")
print(message)
```

**Output:** "Start of the work week"

**3.2 Looping Statements:** These statements allow you to repeat a block of code multiple times.

**3.2.1 for loop:** It is a control flow statement for specifying iteration, which allows code to be executed repeatedly. The for loop is typically used when the number of iterations is known before entering the loop. It is one of the most commonly used loops in programming for iterating over a sequence (such as a list, vector, or range).

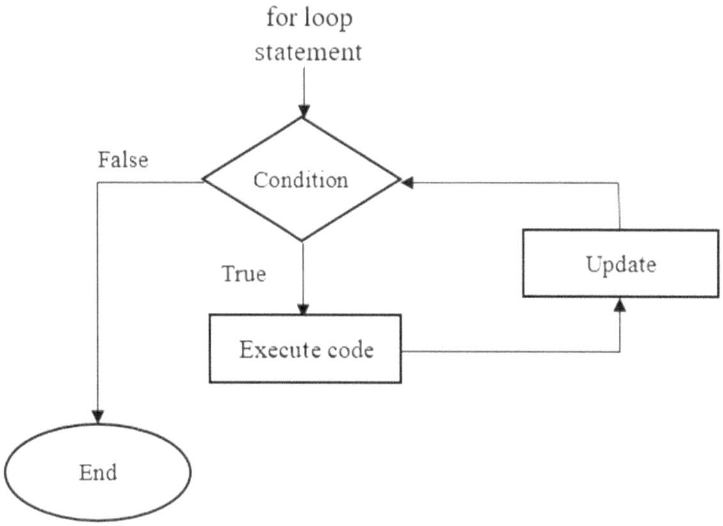

- **Syntax :**

```
for (variable in sequence) {
 # block of code to be executed
}
```

- Example:

```
for (i in 1:5) {
  print(i)
}
```

**Output:**

```
1
2
3
4
5
```

**3.2.2 While loop:** A **while loop** is a control flow statement that allows code to be executed repeatedly based on a given boolean condition. The while loop can be used when the number of iterations is not known beforehand and should continue running as long as the specified condition remains true.

- **Syntax:**

```
while (condition) {
 # block of code to be executed
}
```

- **Example:**

```
i <- 1
while (i <= 5) {
  print(i)
  i <- i + 1
}
```

**Output:**

```
1
2
3
4
5
```

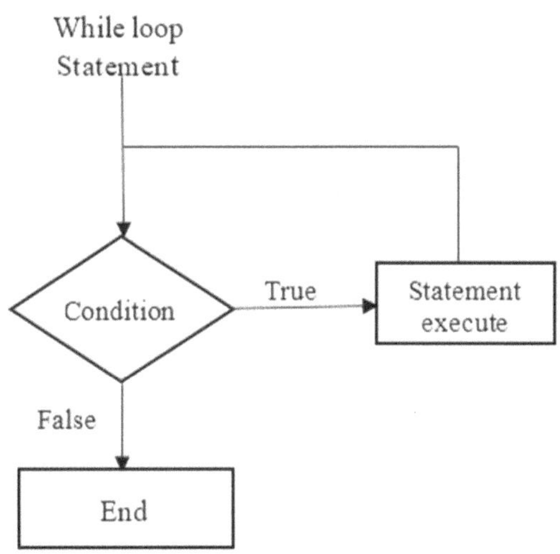

**3.2.3 Repeat Loop:** A repeat loop in R repeatedly executes a block of code until a specified condition is met. Unlike other loops, it has no built-in stop condition and relies on an explicit break statement to exit, running indefinitely until the break condition is satisfied.

- **Syntax:**

```
repeat {
  # Code to execute
  if (condition) {
    break
  }
}
```

- **Example:**

```
i <- 1
repeat {
  print(i)
  i <- i + 1
  if (i > 5) {
    break
  }
}

Output:
1
2
3
4
5
```

### 3.3 Jump Statements

It allow you to control the flow of loops and functions by breaking out of loops, skipping iterations, or returning from functions.

**3.3.1 break Statement:** The break statement is used to exit a loop prematurely. When break is encountered inside a loop, the loop is terminated immediately, and control is transferred to the first statement following the loop.

- **Syntax:**

```
break
```

- **Example:**

```
for (i in 1:10) {
  if (i == 5) {
    break
  }
  print(i)
}

Output:
1
2
3
4
```

### 3.3.2 next Statement

The next statement is used to skip the current iteration of a loop and proceed to the next iteration. When next is encountered, the remaining code inside the loop for the current iteration is skipped, and the loop proceeds with the next iteration.

- **Syntax:**

```
next
```

- **Example:**

```
for (i in 1:10) {
  if (i == 5) {
    next
  }
  print(i)
}

Output:
1
2
3
4
5
6
7
8
9
10
```

## 3.4 Functions in R

Functions are self-contained **blocks of code** designed to perform a specific task. They can take inputs, process those inputs, and return outputs. Functions are fundamental for organizing and reusing code, enabling more readable and maintainable scripts.

**Creating a Function**

To create a function in R, you use the **function keyword** followed by parentheses for parameters and curly braces {} for the function body.

- Syntax:

```
function_name <- function(arguments) {
    # Function body
    # Code to execute
}
```

**Parameters or Arguments in functions**

Parameters (or arguments) in functions are variables that are passed to a function to provide input data for processing. They allow functions to operate on different data each time they are called.

**Types of Parameters**

- **Positional Arguments**: The most common type of parameters, where the order of the arguments passed to the function matters.
- **Default Arguments**: Parameters that have default values. If the caller does not provide a value for these parameters, the default value is used.
- **Named Arguments:** Also known as keyword arguments, where each argument is explicitly named in the function call, making the order irrelevant.
- **Variable-length Arguments:** Using ... to allow a function to accept a variable number of arguments.

**Calling a function**

To call a function, you use the function name followed by parentheses (). If the function requires arguments, you pass them inside the parentheses.

- Example:

```
function_name(argument1, argument2, ...)
```

### 3.5 Actual Arguments

Actual arguments are the specific values or variables passed to a function when it is called. These arguments match the parameters defined in the function definition and are used within the function's body.

- Example:

- **Example:**

```
add <- function(a, b) {
   sum <- a + b
   return(sum)
 }

result <- add(3, 5)        <---- Call the function with arguments
print(result)

Output: 8
```

### 3.6 Named Arguments

Named arguments allow you to explicitly specify which value should be assigned to which parameter, enhancing code readability and flexibility. This is particularly useful for functions with many parameters.

- Example:

```
info <- function(name, age, city) {
  print(paste("Name:", name))
  print(paste("Age:", age))
  print(paste("City:", city))
}
info(name = "Martha", city = "Jaipur", age = 30)
```

**Output:**

```
"Name: Martha"
"Age: 30"
"City: Jaipur"
```

### 3.7 Global and Local Variables

**Global variables** are defined in the main body of the R script and can be accessed from anywhere within the script.

**Local variables** are defined within a function and are only accessible within that function's scope.

- **Example:**

```
# Global variable
global_var <- "I am global"
my_function <- function() {

# Local variable
local_var <- "I am local"
print(local_var)
print(global_var)        <---- Accessing global variable within a function
}
```

```
my_function()
print(global_var)
# print(local_var)

Output:
#my_function()
"I am local"
"I am global"
# print(global_var)
"I am global"
```

This will give an error because local_var is not accessible outside the function

### 3.8 Argument and Lazy Evaluation

In R, lazy evaluation means that function arguments are not evaluated until they are actually used within the function. This can help in optimizing performance and preventing unnecessary computations.

- Example:

```
# Define a function
lazy_evaluation_example <- function(x, y) {
print(x)
print("Y will not be evaluated if not used")
}
 # Call the function
lazy_evaluation_example(10, stop("This will not stop the execution")
)
```

**Output:**

```
10
"Y will not be evaluated if not used"
```

### 3.9 Recursive Function

A recursive function is one that calls itself within its definition. Recursive functions are particularly useful for tasks that can be defined in terms of similar subtasks.

- Example:

```
# Define a function
lazy_evaluation_example <- function(x, y) {
print(x)
print("Y will not be evaluated if not used")
}
 # Call the function
lazy_evaluation_example(10, stop("This will not stop the execution")
)

Output:
10
"Y will not be evaluated if not used"
```

### 3.10 Types of functions in R

**3.10.1 Built-in Functions:** Built-in functions are pre-defined functions provided by the R language and its standard libraries. These functions cover a wide range of operations, including mathematical computations, data manipulation, statistical analysis, and more. They are optimized for performance and designed to handle common tasks efficiently.

**Key Points:**

- **Mathematical Functions:** Perform basic arithmetic operations like sum, mean, and square root.
- **Statistical Functions:** Calculate median, standard deviation, and variance.
- **Character Functions:** Manipulate strings, such as converting to uppercase or extracting substrings.
- **Data Manipulation Functions:** Sort elements, find unique values, and determine the length of vectors.

**Example:**

```
# Define a vector of numbers
numbers <- c(1, 2, 3, 4, 5)
# Calculate the sum of the numbers
total <- sum(numbers)
# Print the result
print(total)
```

**Output:** 15

**3.10.2 User-defined functions:** User-defined functions are custom functions created by users to perform specific tasks. These functions enhance modularity and reusability in code, allowing for better management of complex programs.

**Key Points:**

- **Definition:** Created using the function keyword and encapsulating logic within curly braces {}.
- **Parameters:** Can accept parameters, which can have default values and be specified by name for clarity.
- **Recursion:** Supports recursive calls, allowing functions to call themselves for tasks like calculating factorials.

**Example:**

```
# Define a user-defined function to add two numbers
add_numbers <- function(a, b) {
result <- a + b return(result)
} # Call the user-defined function with actual arguments
sum_result <- add_numbers(10, 5)
# Print the result
print(sum_result)
```

**Output:** 15

**Summary**

- **Control Statements:** Manage the flow of program execution.
- **Conditional Statements:** Execute code based on true/false conditions.
- **Looping Statements:** Repeat code multiple times.
- **Jump Statements:** Alter the flow within loops.
- **Functions:** Blocks of code for specific tasks.
- **Recursive Functions:** Functions calling themselves.
- Built-in Functions: Pre-defined in R.
- **User-defined Functions:** Custom-created functions.

**Glossary**
- **Parameters:** Inputs to functions.
- **Actual Arguments:** Values passed to functions.
- **Named Arguments:** Explicitly named parameter values.
- **Global Variables:** Accessible throughout the script.
- **Local Variables:** Accessible only within the function.
- **Lazy Evaluation:** Evaluate arguments when used.

## Exercises

**Exercise 1 – Multiple Choice Questions**

1. Which statement is used to exit a loop prematurely in R?
   a) continue    b) break
   c) next    d) exit
2. In R, which type of loop is used when the number of iterations is known beforehand?
   a) while loop    b) repeat loop
   c) for loop    d) switch loop

**Exercise 2 – Fill in the blanks**

1. The _______ operator in R is used to combine multiple conditions and evaluate whether at least one of the conditions is true.
2. In R, a _______ loop is a control flow statement that allows code to be executed repeatedly based on a given boolean condition.

**Exercise 3 – True or False**

1. The switch statement in R evaluates an expression and executes the corresponding block of code based on the matched value.
2. The next statement in R is used to exit a loop prematurely.

**Exercise 4 – Short answer type questions**

1. What is the purpose of the `if` statement in R?
2. How do you create a user-defined function in R?

**Exercise 5 – Long answer type questions**

1. Explain the concept of lazy evaluation in R with an example.
2. Describe the different types of control statements in R with examples.

## Answers

**Exercise 1** – 1. b) 2. c)
**Exercise 2** – 1. or 2. while
**Exercise 3** – 1. True 2. False

## Online Resources

**Practice Paper**
**Link:** https://forms.gle/DVrmFk4SuQjZ8VRV7
**QR Code**

**Project video Link**
**Link:** https://www.youtube.com/playlist?list=PLzlh_31VWEFqQ_cS64zGtSbhdGI0d7sUv
**QR Code**

**YouTube Video Playlist Link**
**Link:** https://www.youtube.com/playlist?list=PLzlh_31VWEFqQ_cS64zGtSbhdGI0d7sUv
**QR Code**

**Test Paper**

## Chapter-3
## Control Statements, Loop and Functions

**Time Duration: 40 Minutes** **Maximum Marks: 25**

**General Instructions:**

1. The question paper consists of 12 questions and is divided into four sections, A, B, C and D.
2. All questions are compulsory.
3. Section A comprises MCQs, Fill in the blanks and True or False carrying one marks each.
4. Section B comprises VSAQs(very short answers questions) carrying two marks each.
5. Section C comprises SAQs(short questions) carrying four marks each.
6. Section D comprises long questions carrying five marks each.

### SECTION-A

**I. Multiple choice questions:** **(1*2=2)**

1. Which statement in R is used to evaluate an expression and execute code based on the matched value?
   a) if-else b) for loop
   c) switch d) repeat loop
2. Which logical operator in R is used to combine multiple conditions and evaluate whether both are true?
   a) || b) &&
   c) & d) |

**II. Fill in the blanks:** **(1*2=2)**

1. The operator used to check if one value is greater than another in R is the __________ operator.
2. The %% operator in R returns the __________ of a division.

**III. True or False: (1*2=2)**

1. Global variables in R are defined within a function and are accessible only within that function.
2. The sum() function in R is a user-defined function used to calculate the sum of elements.

### SECTION-B

**IV. Very Short answers type questions-I** **(2*3=6)**

1. What is the primary purpose of using the if statement in R?
2. Name two types of assignment operators in R.
3. What does the break statement do in a loop?

### SECTION-C

**V. Short answers type questions-II** **(4*2=8)**

1. Explain the difference between global and local variables in R.
2. Describe the use of the `switch` statement in R.

### SECTION-D

**VI. Long answers type questions** **(5*1=5)**

1. Discuss the various types of control statements in R and provide examples of each.

# Chapter 4: Vectors

**In this chapter you will learn about:**
**- Create Vector**
**- Access Element of Vector**
**- Operators of Vector**
**- Vector Arithmetic and Manipulation**
**- Deleting a Vector**
**- Vector Element Sorting**

**Vector**
A vector in R is a basic data structure that holds elements of the same type. It is a sequence of data elements, where each element is identified by its position within the vector. Vectors are fundamental in R and are used extensively for data manipulation, statistical analysis, and many other operations.

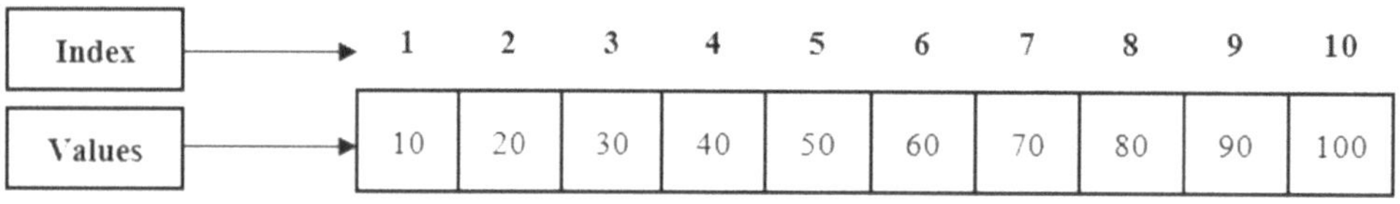


**Characteristics of Vector**
- All elements in a vector must be of the same type (e.g., numeric, character, logical).
- Elements in a vector are accessed using square brackets [] with a 1-based index.
- Vectors can be dynamically resized by adding or removing elements.

**4.1 Types of Vectors**
Vectors in R can hold various types of data, and each type serves specific purposes. The types of vectors in R are:

**1. Numeric Vectors:** Numeric vectors are the most common type of vectors in R and include both integer and floating-point (decimal) numbers.

**Example:**

```
num_vector <- c(1.5, 2.8, 3.3, 4.0)   ← Double
print(num_vector)
```

**Output:** 1.5 2.8 3.3 4.0

**2. Integer Vectors:** Integer vectors specifically contain integer values. The values are created by appending an L to the numbers.
**Example:**

```
int_vector <- c(1L, 2L, 3L, 4L)
print(int_vector)
```

**Output:** 1 2 3 4

**3. Character Vectors:** Character vectors contain string data. Each element in the vector is a character string.
**Example:**

```
char_vector <- c("apple", "banana", "cherry")
print(char_vector)
```

**Output:** "apple" "banana" "cherry"

**4. Logical Vectors:** Logical vectors consist of boolean values (TRUE or FALSE).
**Example:**

```
logical_vector <- c(TRUE, FALSE, TRUE, FALSE)
print(logical_vector)
```

**Output:** TRUE FALSE TRUE FALSE

**5. Complex Vectors:** Complex vectors contain complex numbers, which have both real and imaginary parts.
**Example:**

```
complex_vector <- c(1+2i, 3+4i, 5+6i)
print(complex_vector)
```

**Output:** 1+2i 3+4i 5+6i

**6. Factor Vectors:** Factor vectors are used to represent categorical data and are particularly useful in statistical modeling. They can have a fixed set of unique values called levels.
**Example:**

```
factor_vector <- factor(c("low", "medium", "high", "medium"))
print(factor_vector)
```

**Output:** low medium high medium
Levels: high l ow medium

**4.2 Create Vector**

Creating vectors in R is a fundamental task. You can use various functions to create vectors, with c() being the most commonly used function for combining values into a vector.

**1. Using the c() Function:** The c() function (combine or concatenate) is the most common way to create vectors in R.

**Example:**

```
vector <- c(1, 2, 3, 4, 5)
print(vector)
```

**Output:** 1 2 3 4 5

**2. Using the seq() Function:** The seq() function creates a sequence of numbers with specified start, end, and step values.

**Example:**

```
vector <- seq(1, 10, by = 2)
print(vector)
```

**Output:** 1 3 5 7 9

**3. Using the : Operator:** The colon operator (:) creates a sequence of numbers with a step of 1.
**Example:**

```
vector <- seq(1, 10, by = 2)
print(vector)
```

**Output:** 1 3 5 7 9

**3. Using the : Operator:** The colon operator (:) creates a sequence of numbers with a step of 1.
**Example:**

```
vector <- 1:10
print(vector)
```

**Output:** 1 2 3 4 5 6 7 8 9 10

**4. Using the rep() Function:** The rep() function replicates elements of vectors. **Example:**

```
vector <- rep(3,5)
print(vector)
```

**Output:** 3 3 3 3 3

**Multiple Elements Example:**

```
vector <- rep(c(1,2,3), times = 3)
print(vector)
```

**Output:** 1 2 3 1 2 3 1 2 3

**5. Using the numeric(), character(), logical(), and integer() Functions:** These functions create vectors of a specified length, initialized to default values.Examples are shown above.

**6. Combining Different Types (Coercion):** If you combine elements of different types, R coerces them to the most flexible type.
**Example:**

```
vector <- c(1, "apple", TRUE)
print(vector)
```

**Output:** "1" "apple" "TRUE"

### 4.3 Access Vector

Accessing elements of a vector in R can be done in several ways, depending on what you need. Here's a different methods to access vector elements:

```
vector <- c(10, 20, 30, 40, 50)
```

**1. Single Element Access:** To access a single element, use square brackets [] with the position (index) of the element you want to retrieve. Note that R uses 1-based indexing, so the first element is at index 1.
**Example:**

```
element_3 <- vector[3]
print(element_3)
```

**Output:** 30

**2. Multiple Elements Access:** To access multiple elements, use a vector of indices inside the square brackets.
**Example:**

```
elements_2_and_4 <- vector[c(2, 4)]
print(elements_2_and_4)
```

**Output:** 20 40

**3. Range of Elements Access:** To access a range of elements, use the : operator to create a sequence of indices.
**Example:**

```
elements_2_to_5 <- vector[2:5]
print(elements_2_to_5)
```

**Output:** 20 30 40 50

**4. Excluding Specific Elements:** To access all elements except certain ones, use the negative indices of the elements you want to exclude.
**Example:**

```
exclude_element_3 <- vector[-3]
print(exclude_element_3)
```

**Output:** 10 20 40 50

**5. Logical Indexing:** Logical vectors can be used to access elements that meet certain conditions.
**Example:**

```
elements_greater_than_25 <- vector[vector > 25]
print(elements_greater_than_25)
```

**Output:** 30 40 50

**6. Name-based Access:** If your vector elements have names, you can access them using these names.
**Example:**

```
named_vector <- c(a = 10, b = 20, c = 30)
element_b <- named_vector["b"]
print(element_b)
```

**Output:** 20

**7. Access Using which Function:** The which function can be used to find the indices of elements that satisfy a condition.
**Example:**

```
indices_greater_than_25 <- which(vector > 25)
print(indices_greater_than_25)
```

**Output:** 3 4 5

```
elements_by_condition <- vector[indices_greater_than_25]
print(elements_by_condition)
```

**Output:** 30 40 50

**8. Access Using Logical Vectors:** Logical vectors can directly index elements that are TRUE.
**Example:**

```
logical_vector <- c(TRUE, FALSE, TRUE, FALSE, TRUE)
elements_by_logical_vector <- vector[logical_vector]
print(elements_by_logical_vector)
```

**Output:** 10 30 50

**9. Vector Recycling:** When accessing elements using a shorter vector, R will recycle the shorter vector to match the length of the longer vector.
**Example:**

```
short_logical_vector <- c(TRUE, FALSE)
elements_by_recycling <- vector[short_logical_vector]
print(elements_by_recycling)
```

**Output:** 10 30 50

**4.4 Delete Vector**

Deleting a vector in R involves removing its reference from the environment so that the memory it occupies can be freed up. Here's a detailed explanation:

**1. Using rm() Function:** The rm() function is used to remove objects, including vectors, from the R environment

- Deleting a Single Vector:

**Example:**

```
vector <- c(1, 2, 3, 4, 5)
rm(vector)
# Check if the vector is deleted
exists("mvector")
```

**Output**: FALSE

- Deleting Multiple Vectors:

**Example:**

```
vector <- c(1, 2, 3, 4, 5)
rm(vector)
# Check if the vector is deleted
exists("mvector")
```

**Output**: FALSE

**2. Using remove() Function:** The remove() function is an alias for rm(). It works the same way:

- Deleting a Single Vector:

**Example:**

```
vector <- c(1, 2, 3, 4, 5)
remove(vector)
# Check if the vector is deleted
exists("vector")
```

**Output:** TRUE

- Deleting Multiple Vectors:

**Example:**

```
vector1 <- c(1, 2, 3)
vector2 <- c(4, 5, 6)
remove(vector1, vector2)
exists("vector1")
exists("vector2")
```

**Output:** FALSE FALSE

**3. Using assign() and NULL:** Another way to effectively "delete" a vector is to assign it NULL, which removes its data and frees up memory:

- Assigning NULL to a Vector:

```
vector <- c(1, 2, 3, 4, 5)
vector <- NULL
# Check if the vector is empty
is.null(vector)
```

**Output:** TRUE

**4. Removing All Objects from Environment:** If you want to clear the entire environment, including all vectors and other objects, you can use the rm(list = ls()) command:

- Remove All Objects:

```
vector1 <- c(1, 2, 3)
vector2 <- c(4, 5, 6)
rm(list = ls())
# Check if the environment is empty
ls()
```

**Output:** character(0)

### 4.5 Sorting Vectors

Sorting vectors in R is a fundamental operation in data manipulation and analysis. Here's a detailed explaination:

#### 4.5.1 Basic Sorting

**- Sorting in Ascending Order:**The sort() function is used to sort elements of a vector in ascending order by default.

```
vector <- c(3, 1, 4, 1, 5, 9, 2)
sorted_vector <- sort(vector)
print(sorted_vector)
```

**Output:** 1 1 2 3 4 5 9

**- Sorting in Descending Order:** To sort elements in descending order, use the decreasing parameter and set it to TRUE.

```
vector <- c(3, 1, 4, 1, 5, 9, 2)
sorted_vector_desc <- sort(vector, decreasing = TRUE)
print(sorted_vector_desc)
```

**Output:** 9 5 4 3 2 1 1

**4.5.2 Sorting Character Vectors:** Character vectors can also be sorted alphabetically:

**Example:**

```
vector <- c("banana", "apple", "cherry", "date")
sorted_char_vector <- sort(vector)
print(sorted_char_vector)
```

**Output:** "apple" "banana" "cherry" "date"

**4.5.3 Sorting Logical Vectors:** Logical vectors are sorted with FALSE coming before TRUE:

**Example:**

```
vector <- c(TRUE, FALSE, TRUE, FALSE)
sorted_logical_vector <- sort(vector)
print(sorted_logical_vector)
```

**Output:** FALSE FALSE TRUE TRUE

**4.5.4 Using order() Function:** The order() function returns the indices that would sort the vector. This is useful for sorting related vectors based on one vector's ordering.

- Getting Order Indices:

```
vector <- c(3, 1, 4, 1, 5, 9, 2)
```

```
order_indices <- order(vector)
print(order_indices)
```

**Output:** 2 4 7 1 3 5 6

- Using Order Indices to Sort:

```
vector <- c(3, 1, 4, 1, 5, 9, 2)
sorted_by_indices <- vector[order_indices]
print(sorted_by_indices)
```

**Output:** 1 1 2 3 4 5 9

- **Sorting Multiple Vectors:** If you have related vectors and you want to sort them based on one vector's order:

```
vector_a <- c(5, 2, 8, 3)
vector_b <- c("e", "b", "h", "c")
order_indices <- order(vector_a)
sorted_vector_a <- vector_a[order_indices]
sorted_vector_b <- vector_b[order_indices]
print(sorted_vector_a)
print(sorted_vector_b)
```

**Output:** 2 3 5 8
"b" "c" "e" "h"

**4.5.5 Sorting with rank():** The rank() function gives the ranks of the elements, which can be used to sort the vector by rank:

```
vector <- c(3, 1, 4, 1, 5, 9, 2)
ranks <- rank(vector)
sorted_by_rank <- vector[order(ranks)]
print(sorted_by_rank)
```

**Output:** 2 3 5 8
"b" "c" "e" "h"

**4.5.6 Sorting with sort.int() and sort.list():** These functions are lower-level and slightly more efficient for sorting large vectors.

- sort.int():

```
vector <- c(3, 1, 4, 1, 5, 9, 2)
sorted_int <- sort.int(vector)
print(sorted_int)
```

**Output:** 1 1 2 3 4 5 9

- sort.list():

```
sorted_list <- sort.list(vector)
sorted_by_list <- vector[sorted_list]
print(sorted_by_list)
```

**Output:** 1 1 2 3 4 5 9

**4.5.7 Handling NA Values:** By default, sort() places NA values at the end of the vector. You can control this behavior using the na.last parameter:

- NA Values Last (Default):

```
vector_na <- c(3, NA, 1, 4, NA, 2)
sorted_na_last <- sort(vector_na, na.last = TRUE)
```

```
print(sorted_na_last)
```

**Output:** 1 2 3 4 NA NA

- NA Values First:

```
vector_na <- c(3, NA, 1, 4, NA, 2)
sorted_na_last_first <- sort(vector_na, na.last = FALSE)
print(sorted_na_last_first)
```

**Output:** NA NA 1 2 3 4

- Remove NA Values:

```
vector_na <- c(3, NA, 1, 4, NA, 2)
sorted_na_last_first <- sort(vector_na, na.last = NA)
print(sorted_na_last_first)
```

**Output:** 1 2 3 4

## Glossary

- **Vector:** A sequence of elements of the same type.
- **Numeric Vector:** Contains integer and floating-point numbers.
- **Character Vector:** Contains string data.
- **Logical Vector:** Contains boolean values.
- **Complex Vector:** Contains complex numbers.
- **Factor Vector:** Represents categorical data with levels.
- **c() Function:** Combines values into a vector.
- **seq() Function:** Creates a sequence of numbers.
- **: Operator:** Creates a sequence with a step of 1.

## Summary

- **rep() Function:** Replicates elements of vectors.
- **Coercion:** Converts elements to the most flexible type.
- **Indexing:** Accessing vector elements with square brackets.
- **Logical Indexing:** Uses logical vectors to filter elements.
- **rm() Function:** Removes objects from the environment.
- **sort() Function:** Sorts elements of a vector.
- **order() Function:** Returns indices for sorting.
- **NA Values:** Missing values in a vector.

# Exercises

**Exercise 1 – Multiple Choice Questions**

1. Which function in R is commonly used to create vectors by combining elements?
   a) seq()  b) rep()
   c) c()  d) order()
2. What will be the result of the following R code: sort(c(3, 1, 4, NA, 2), na.last = FALSE)?
   a) 1 2 3 4 NA  b) NA 1 2 3 4
   c) 4 3 2 1 NA  d) 1 2 3 4

**Exercise 2 - Fill in the Blanks**

1. To create a sequence of numbers from 1 to 10 in R, you can use the ________ operator.
2. The ________ function in R returns the indices that would sort the vector.

**Exercise 3 - True or False**

1. Logical vectors in R can contain elements other than TRUE and FALSE.

2. The rm() function in R can be used to delete multiple vectors from the environment.

**Exercise 4 - Short Answer Questions**
1. How can you sort a character vector in descending order in R?
2. What is vector recycling in R?

**Exercise 5 - Long Answer Questions**
1. Explain the different ways to create vectors in R, providing examples for each method.
2. Discuss the methods for accessing vector elements in R, including examples for each method.

## Answers

**Exercise 1** – 1. c) 2. b)
**Exercise 2** – 1. colon (:) 2. order()
**Exercise 3** – 1. False 2. True

### Online Resources

**Practice Paper**
**Link:** https://forms.gle/Dj1XJFPuqxwRriXz7
**QR Code**

**Project Video**
**Link:** https://www.youtube.com/playlist?list=PLzlh_31VWEFqLncqufM2GqPLSFRoSejV-
**QR Code**

**YouTube Video Playlist Link**
**Link**
https://www.youtube.com/playlist?list=PLzlh_31VWEFqLncqufM2GqPLSFRoSejV-
**QR Code**

**Test Paper**
**Chapter-4**

## Vectors

**Time Duration: 40 Minutes** **Maximum Marks: 25**

**General Instructions:**

1. The question paper consists of 12 questions and is divided into four sections, A, B, C and D.
2. All questions are compulsory.
3. Section A comprises MCQs, Fill in the blanks and True or False carrying one marks each.
4. Section B comprises VSAQs(very short answers questions) carrying two marks each.
5. Section C comprises SAQs(short questions) carrying four marks each.
6. Section D comprises long questions carrying five marks each.

### SECTION-A

**I. Multiple choice questions:** **(1*2=2)**

1. Which function in R can create a sequence of numbers from 1 to 10?
   a) seq() b) rep()
   c) c() d) order()
2. What does the rep() function in R do?
   a) Sorts a vector
   b) Combines elements into a vector
   c) Creates a sequence of numbers
   d) Replicates elements of a vector

**II. Fill in the blanks:** **(1*2=2)**

1. The function used to remove objects, including vectors, from the R environment is ________.
2. To access a range of elements in a vector, you can use the ________ operator to create a sequence of indices.

**III. True or False:** **(1*2=2)**

1. Character vectors in R can be sorted alphabetically.
2. The which function in R returns the indices of elements that satisfy a specified condition.

### SECTION-B

**IV. Very Short answers type questions-I** **(2*3=6)**

1. What does the rep() function do in R?
2. How do you remove a vector named my_vector from the R environment?
3. How can you access the third element of a vector named my_vector in R?

### SECTION-C

**V. Short answers type questions-II** **(4*2=8)**

1. How can you create a numeric vector with values from 1 to 10 using the seq() function in R?
2. Explain how the order() function can be used to sort a related vector based on another vector's ordering.

### SECTION-D

**VI. Long answers type questions** **(5*1=5)**

1. Discuss the different methods for creating vectors in R, including examples for each method.

# Chapter 5: Lists

**In this chapter you will learn about:- Creating a List**
**- Naming a List**
**- Accessing and Updating List Element**
**- Sorting and Searching**
**- Merging List**
**- List to Vector Conversion**

## Lists

A list in R is a flexible and versatile data structure that can hold multiple elements of different types and structures. Unlike vectors, which are constrained to elements of the same type, lists can include elements such as numbers, strings, vectors, matrices, and even other lists. This makes lists particularly useful for grouping related but heterogeneous data.

**Characteristics of Lists in R**

- Lists can contain elements of varying types, including numeric, character, logical, complex, and other lists.
- Elements in a list are accessed using double square brackets `[[ ]]` for single elements and single square brackets `[]` for sublists.
- Lists can have named elements, allowing for more intuitive access.
- Lists can be dynamically resized, meaning you can add or remove elements as needed.

### 5.1 Types of Lists in R

**1. Homogeneous Lists:** These lists contain elements of the same type. While lists are generally used for heterogeneous data, homogeneous lists can be useful in certain scenarios.

**Example:**

```
list <- list(1, 2, 3, 4)   # ← All elements are numeric
print(list)
```

**Output:**

```
1
2
3
4
```

**2. Heterogeneous Lists:** These lists contain elements of different types, such as numbers, strings, logical values, vectors, and even other lists.

**Example:**

```
list <- list(1, "apple", TRUE, c(1, 2, 3))
print(list)
```

**Output:**

```
1
"apple"
"TRUE"
1 2 3
```

**3. Named Lists:** These lists have named elements, which can be accessed using the names. Naming the elements can make the list easier to work with.

**Example:**

```
list <- list(number = 1, fruit = "apple", is_true =TRUE, c(1, 2, 3))
print(list)
```

**Output:**

```
1
"apple"
"TRUE"
1 2 3
```

**4. Nested Lists:** These are lists within lists. Nested lists are useful for representing hierarchical data structures.

**Example:**

```
list <- list(a = list(1, 2, 3), b = list("apple", "banana"))
print(list)
```

**Output:**

```
1
2
3
"apple"
"banana"
```

**5. Recursive Lists:** These lists are similar to nested lists but can include the list itself as an element, making them recursive. This is less common but can be useful in specific applications.

**Example:**

```
list <- list(a = 1)
list$b <- list
print(list)
```

**Output:**

```
1
1
```

**6. Empty Lists:** These lists are initialized without any elements. You can add elements to them later.

**Example:**

```
list <- list(a = 1)
list$b <- list
print(list)
```

**Output:**

```
1
1
```

### 5.2 Creating Lists in R

A list in R is a flexible and powerful data structure that can contain elements of different types, including numbers, strings, vectors, and even other lists. Here are several methods to create lists in R with examples:

**1. Basic List Creation:** You can create a simple list containing various types of elements using the list() function.

**Example:**

```
list <- list(42, "apple", TRUE, c(1, 2, 3))
print(list)
```

**Output:**

42
"apple"
"TRUE"
1 2 3

**2. Named List Creation:** You can assign names to the elements in a list when you create it. This makes it easier to access elements by their names.

**Example:**

```
list <- list(number = 42, fruit = "apple", is_true = TRUE, c(1, 2, 3))
print(list)
```

**Output:**

42
"apple"
"TRUE"
1 2 3

**3. Using names() Function to Name Elements:** You can create a list first and then assign names to its elements using the names() function.

**Example:**

```
list <- list(number = 42, fruit = "apple", is_true = TRUE, c(1, 2, 3))
print(list)
```

**Output:**

42
"apple"
"TRUE"
1 2 3

← Create a list and then assign names to its elements

**4. Creating Lists from Existing Vectors:** You can create lists from existing vectors or other data structures.

**Example:**

```
vector1 <- c(1, 2, 3)                        ← Create Vectors
vector2 <- c("one", "two", "three")
combined_list <- list(vector1, vector2)      ← Create a list from these vectors
print(combined_list)
```

**Output:**

1 2 3
"one" "two" "three"

**5. Combining Lists:** You can combine multiple lists into a single list using the c() function.

**Example:**

```
list1 <- list(a = 1, b = 2)                  ← Create two lists
list2 <- list(c = 3, d = 4)
combined_list <- c(list1, list2)             ← Combine the lists into one
print(combined_list)
```

**Output:**

1
2
3
4

**5.3 Accessing Elements in R:** Accessing elements within a list in R can be done using various methods, including by index, by name, and by logical conditions. Here's a detailed guide on how to access and manipulate list elements in R:

**1. Accessing by Index:** To access elements in a list by their position, use double square brackets [[ ]] or single square brackets [ ]:

- Single Element:

**Example:**

```
list <- list(1, "apple", TRUE, c(1, 2, 3))
second_element <- list[[2]]
print(second_element)
```

**Output:**

"apple"

- Multiple Elements (Returns a Sublist):

**Example:**

```
list <- list(1, "apple", TRUE, c(1, 2, 3))
sublist <- list[c(1, 3)]
print(sublist)
```

**Output:** 1 TRUE

**2. Accessing by Name:** If the list elements are named, you can access them using the $ operator or double square brackets with the name as a string:

- Using $ Operator:

**Example:**

```
list <- list(number = 1, fruit = "apple", is_true = TRUE)
fruit_element <- list$fruit
print(fruit_element)
```

**Output:** "apple"

- Using Double Square Brackets:

**Example:**

```
list <- list(number = 1, fruit = "apple", is_true = TRUE)
fruit_element <- list[["fruit"]]
print(fruit_element)
```

**Output:** "apple"

**3. Accessing Multiple Elements by Name:** You can access multiple elements by specifying their names in a vector within single square brackets. This will return a sublist:

- Example:

```
list <- list(number = 1, fruit = "apple", is_true = TRUE)
selected_elements <- list[c("number", "is_true")]
print(selected_elements)
```

**Output:**

1

"TRUE"

**4. Accessing Elements by Logical Indexing:** Logical vectors can be used to access elements that meet certain conditions. This method is less common for lists compared to vectors but is still useful:

- Example:

```
list <- list(a = 1, b = 2, c = 3, d = 4)
logical_index <- c(TRUE, FALSE, TRUE, FALSE)
selected_elements <- list[logical_index]
print(selected_elements)
```

**Output:**

```
1
3
```

**5. Accessing Elements with the which Function:** The which function can be used to find the indices of elements that satisfy a condition, which can then be used to access those elements in the list:
- Example:

```
list <- list(a = 1, b = 2, c = 3, d = 4)
indices <- which(sapply(list, function(x) x > 2))
selected_elements <- list[indices]
print(selected_elements)
```

**Output:**

```
3
4
```

**6. Nested Lists:** For lists within lists (nested lists), you can access elements by chaining the [[ ]] operators:
- Example:

```
list <- list(a = list(1, 2, 3), b = list("x", "y", "z"))
first_element_of_a <- list$a[[1]]
print(first_element_of_a)
```

**Output:**

```
1
```

### 5.4 Updating Elements in List

Updating elements in a list in R can be done using various methods depending on whether you are updating a single element, multiple elements, or adding new elements.

#### 5.4.1 Updating by Index

- **Single Element:**

```
list <- list(1, "apple", TRUE, c(1, 2, 3))
list[[2]] <- "banana"
print(list)

Output:
1
"banana"
TRUE
1 2 3
```

Updates the second element

- **Multiple Elements:**

```
list <- list(1, "apple", TRUE, c(1, 2, 3))
list[2:3] <- list("banana", FALSE)
print(list)

Output:
1
"banana"
TRUE
1 2 3
```

Updates the second and third element

### 5.4.2 Updating by Name

- Single Named Element:

```
list <- list(number = 1, fruit = "apple", is_true = TRUE, numbers = c(1, 2, 3))
list$fruit <- "banana"  # Updates the element named 'fruit'
print(list)

Output:
1
"banana"
TRUE
1 2 3
```

Updates the element named fruit

- Multiple Named Elements:

```
list <- list(number = 1, fruit = "apple", is_true = TRUE, numbers = c(1, 2, 3))
list[c("fruit", "is_true")] <- list("banana", FALSE)
print(list)

Output:
1
"banana"
TRUE
1 2 3
```

Updates 'fruit' and 'is true'

### 5.4.3 Using Double Brackets [[ ]]

- Update by Index:

```
list <- list(1, "apple", TRUE, c(1, 2, 3))
list[[2]] <- "banana
print(list)

Output:
1
"banana"
TRUE
1 2 3
```

Updates the second element

- Update by Name:

```
list <- list(number = 1, fruit = "apple", is_true = TRUE, numbers = c(1, 2, 3))
list[["fruit"]] <- "banana"  # Updates the element named 'fruit'
print(my_list)

Output:
1
"banana"
TRUE
1 2 3
```

Updates the element named 'fruit'

### 5.4.4 Adding New Elements to a List

- Using $ to Add a Named Element:

```
my_list <- list (number = 1, fruit = "apple", is_true = TRUE)
my_list$new_element <- "new"       ← Adds a new element named 'new_element'
print(my_list)
```

**Output:**
1
"banana"
TRUE
1 2 3

- Using [[ ]] to Add an Element:

```
list <- list(number = 1, fruit = "apple", is_true = TRUE)
list[["new_element"]] <- "new"       ← Adds a new element named 'new_element'
print(list)
```

**Output:**
1
"apple"
TRUE
"new"

**5.5 Sorting and searching in Lists**

In R, lists can contain heterogeneous elements, which makes sorting a bit more complex compared to vectors. Sorting is generally applied to specific elements within the list that are of a type that supports ordering, such as numeric vectors or character strings. Searching within lists can be performed using various functions to locate elements that meet specific conditions.

**5.5.1 Sorting Elements in a List**

Since lists can contain different types of elements, you typically sort specific elements within the list that are sortable, such as numeric or character vectors.

- **Sorting Numeric Elements:** If a list element is a numeric vector, you can sort it using the sort() function.

```
list <- list(numbers = c(5, 2, 9, 1, 5, 6))
sorted_numbers <- sort(list$numbers)
print(sorted_numbers)
```

**Output:** 1 2 5 5 6 9

- **Sorting Character Elements:** Similarly, if a list element is a character vector, you can sort it alphabetically.

```
list <- list(fruits = c("banana", "apple", "cherry"))
sorted_fruits <- sort(list$fruits)
print(sorted_fruits)
```

**Output:** "apple" "banana" "cherry"

- **Sorting a List of Lists:** If you have a list of lists, you can sort them based on a specific criterion within the sublists.

```
list <- list(list(name = "John", age = 25), list(name = "Alice", age = 30), list(name = "Bob",
age = 20))
sorted_list <- list[order(sapply(list, function(x) x$age))]
print(sorted_list)
```

Output:
"Bob" 20
"John" 25
"Alice" 30

**5.5.2 Searching Elements in a List:** Searching within a list can be done using functions like which(), grep(), or custom conditions.

**- Using which() to Find Elements:** The which() function can be used to find the indices of elements in a vector that satisfy a condition.

```
list <- list(numbers = c(5, 2, 9, 1, 5, 6))
indices <- which(list$numbers == 5)
print(indices)
```

**Output:** 1 5

**- Using grep() to Search Character Elements:** The grep() function can be used to search for patterns in character vectors.

```
list <- list(fruits = c("banana", "apple", "cherry"))
indices <- grep("a", list$fruits)
print(indices)
```

**Output:** 1 2

**- Using Custom Conditions:** You can use custom conditions with sapply() or lapply() to search for elements within a list.

```
list <- list(list(name = "John", age = 25), list(name = "Alice", age = 30), list(name = "Bob",
age = 20))
names_starting_with_A <- sapply(list, function(x) grepl("^A", x$name))
matching_elements <- list[names_starting_with_A]
print(matching_elements)
```

**Output:** "Alice"
30

**5.6 Merging Lists in R**

Merging lists in R is a common task when you need to combine multiple lists into a single list. This can be useful in various scenarios, such as combining data from different sources or appending additional information to an existing list. Here's a detailed guide on how to merge lists in R:

**- Basic Merging of Lists:** To merge two or more lists, you can use the c() function, which concatenates the lists:

```
# Creating two lists
list1 <- list(a = 1, b = 2)
list2 <- list(c = 3, d = 4)

# Merging lists using c() function
merged_list <- c(list1, list2)
# Display the merged list
print(merged_list)
```

**Output:**
1
2
3
4

**- Merging Lists with Duplicate Names:** When merging lists that contain elements with the same names, the c() function will combine them without changing their names:

```
# Creating two lists
list1 <- list(a = 1, b = 2)
list2 <- list(c = 3, d = 4)

# Merging lists using c() function
merged_list <- c(list1, list2)
# Display the merged list
print(merged_list)
```

**Output:**

```
1
2
3
4
```

In this case, the merged list will have multiple elements with the same name a. You can access them using their positions:

```
print(merged_list[[1]])
print(merged_list[[3]])
```

**Output:**

```
1
3
```

**- Appending Elements to a List:** You can append new elements to an existing list by using the c() function:

```
# Creating two lists
list <- list(a = 1, b = 2)
# Appending a new element
list <- c(list, list(c = 3))
# Display the merged list
print(merged_list)
```

**Output:**

```
1
2
3
```

**- Combining Lists with More Complex Structures:** Lists in R can hold complex structures, including other lists. You can merge these complex structures as well:

```
# Creating complex lists
list1 <- list(a = 1, b = list(ba = 2, bb = 3))
list2 <- list(c = 4, d = list(da = 5, db = 6))

# Merging complex lists
merged_list <- c(list1, list2)

# Display the merged list
print(merged_list)
```

**Output:**

```
1
2
3
4
```

5
6

### 5.7 List to Vector Conversion in R

Converting a list to a vector in R is often necessary when you need a simple, flat structure to perform vectorized operations or for further data manipulation. Here, we will explore various methods to convert a list to a vector, including considerations and examples.

#### 5.7.1 List to Vector Conversion

**- Using unlist():** The most straightforward way to convert a list to a vector is by using the unlist() function. This function flattens a list into a vector, concatenating all its elements.

**1. Basic Conversion:**

```
list <- list(1, 2, 3, 4)
vector <- unlist(list)
print(vector)
```

**Output:**

```
1 2 3 4
```

**2. List with Mixed Types:** If the list contains elements of different types, unlist() will coerce them into a common type. The common type is usually the most flexible one, typically character if there are any string elements.

```
list <- list(1, "apple", TRUE, 2.5)
vector <- unlist(list)
print(vector)
```

**Output:**

```
1 “apple” “TRUE” 2.5
```

**3. Named List:** When converting a named list to a vector, the names are preserved.

```
list <- list(a = 1, b = 2, c = 3)
vector <- unlist(list)
print(vector)
```

**Output:**

```
a b c
1 2 3
```

**4. Nested List:** Unlist() can handle nested lists, flattening them into a single vector.

```
list <- list(a = 1, b = list(c = 2, d = 3))
vector <- unlist(list)
print(vector)
```

**Output:**

```
a b.c c.d
1 2   3
```

**5. Preserving Data Types:** If you want to preserve data types and avoid coercion, ensure that all elements in the list are of the same type.

```
list <- list(1, 2, 3, 4.5)
vector <- unlist(list)
print(vector)
```

**Output:**

```
1.0 2.0 3.0 4.0 5.0
```

### 5.7.2 Handling Special Cases

**1. Empty Lists:** Converting an empty list results in an empty vector.

```
list <- list()
vector <- unlist(list)
print(vector)
```

**Output:**

```
NULL
```

**2. List with NULL Elements:** NULL elements in a list are removed when converting to a vector.

```
list <- list(1, NULL, 3)
vector <- unlist(list)
print(vector)
```

**Output:**

```
1 3
```

**3. List of Lists:** When dealing with lists of lists, unlist() flattens all levels.

```
lists <- list(a = list(b = 1, c = 2), d = list(e = 3, f = 4))
vector <- unlist(lists)
print(vector)
```

**Output:**

```
a.b a.c d .e d.f
1   2   3   4
```

**Summary**

- **List:** A flexible data structure in R that can hold multiple elements of different types.
- **Homogeneous List:** A list containing elements of the same type.
- **Heterogeneous List:** A list containing elements of different types.
- **Named List:** A list with named elements.
- **Nested List:** A list that contains other lists as its elements.
- **Recursive List:** A list that includes itself as an element.
- **Empty List:** A list initialized without any elements.
- **Indexing:** Accessing elements in a list using their position.

**Glossary**

- **Logical Indexing:** Using logical conditions to access elements in a list.
- **Sorting:** Arranging elements in a specific order (ascending or descending).
- **Searching:** Finding elements in a list that meet specific conditions.
- **Merging:** Combining multiple lists into a single list.
- **Unlist():** A function that converts a list to a vector.
- **Coercion:** The process of converting elements to a common type when combining different types.

## Exercises

**Exercise 1- Multiple choice questions**

1. Which function is used to create a list in R?
   a) list() b) c()
   c) seq() d) rep()
2. How can you access a named element in a list?
   a) list[element] b) list$element
   c) list[element]$ d) list[[element]]

**Exercise 2 – Fill in the blanks**

1. To combine multiple lists into one, you can use the __________ function.
2. The __________ function flattens a list into a vector, concatenating all its elements.

**Exercise 3 – True or False**
1. Lists in R can be dynamically resized by adding or removing elements.
2. The which() function can be used to find the indices of elements in a list that satisfy a condition.

**Exercise 4 – Short answer questions**
1. How can you merge two lists list1 and list2 into a single list in R? Provide an example.
2. What are the main characteristics of lists in R that distinguish them from vectors?

**Exercise 5 – Long answer questions**
1. Describe in detail how to access and update elements in a list by index and by name, including how to access multiple elements and use logical indexing. Provide examples.

2. Explain the process of converting a list to a vector in R using the unlist() function. Discuss how unlist() handles different types of lists, including mixed-type lists, nested lists, and named lists. Provide examples for each case

# Answers

**Exercise 1** – 1. a) 2. b)
**Exercise 2** – 1. c() 2. Unlist()
**Exercise 3** – 1. True 2. True

**Online Resources**

**Practice Paper**
**Link** https://forms.gle/VtJPb9U6EZU8XTA57
**QR Code**

**Project Video**
**Link:** https://www.youtube.com/playlist?list=PLzlh_31VWEFp3OchKlozdoioCmNZ2TcBp
**QR Code**

**YouTube Video Playlist Link**

**Link**
https://www.youtube.com/playlist?list=PLzlh_31VWEFp3OchKlozdoioCmNZ2TcBp
**QR Code**

**Test Paper**
**Chapter-5**
**Lists**

**Time Duration: 40 Minutes** **Maximum Marks: 25**

**General Instructions:**
1. The question paper consists of 12 questions and is divided into four sections, A, B, C and D.
2. All questions are compulsory.
3. Section A comprises MCQs, Fill in the blanks and True or False carrying one marks each.
4. Section B comprises VSAQs(very short answers questions) carrying two marks each.
5. Section C comprises SAQs(short questions) carrying four marks each.
6. Section D comprises long questions carrying five marks each.

## SECTION-A

**I. Multiple choice questions:** **(1*2=2)**

1. What will be the result of unlist(list(a = 1, b = "apple", c = TRUE))?
   a) 1 "apple" TRUE  b) "1" "apple" "TRUE"
   c) 1 2 3  d) a b c
2. How do you update the second element of a list named my_list to "banana"?
   a) my_list[2] <- "banana"  b) my_list[[2]] <- "banana"
   c) my_list$2 <- "banana"  d) my_list["2"] <- "banana"

**II. Fill in the blanks:** **(1*2=2)**

1. To combine multiple lists into one, you can use the __________ function.
2. The __________ function flattens a list into a vector, concatenating all its elements.

**III. True or False:** **(1*2=2)**

1. A list in R can only contain elements of the same type.
2. The names() function is used to assign names to elements of a list after its creation.

## SECTION-B

**IV. Very Short answers type questions-I** **(2*3=6)**

1. How do you create a list with elements 1, "apple", and TRUE in R?
2. What does the unlist() function do in R?
3. How can you add a new named element "color" with the value "blue" to a list named my_list?

## SECTION-C

**V. Short answers type questions-II** **(4*2=8)**

1. Explain the difference between homogeneous lists and heterogeneous lists in R, providing an example for each.
2. Describe how to access the second element of a nested list in R.

## SECTION-D

**VI. Long answers type questions** **(5*1=5)**

1. Discuss the various methods for creating lists in R, including basic list creation, named lists, and lists from existing vectors. Provide examples for each method0

# Chapter 6: Matrix

**In this chapter you will learn about:**
**- Creating a Matrix**
**- Accessing Matrix Elements**
**- Matrix Arithmetic and manipulation**
**- Matrix Operations**

**Matrix in R**
A matrix in R is a two-dimensional, homogeneous data structure that contains elements of the same type arranged in rows and columns. Matrices are an essential component in R for performing mathematical computations, data analysis, and various operations that require a structured grid of data. Here are the key aspects of matrices in R:

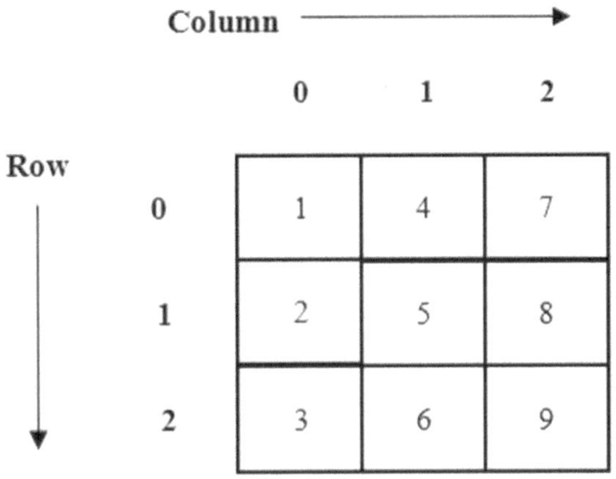


**Key Characteristics of Matrices**
**1. Homogeneous Data Type:** All elements in a matrix must be of the same type (e.g., numeric, character, or logical).
**2. Two-Dimensional Structure:**Matrices have a fixed number of rows and columns, making them a grid-like structure.
**3. Column-Major Order:**Elements in a matrix are filled in column-wise by default. This means the data fills down the columns first and then moves to the next column.

**6.1 Creating Matrix**

**6.1.1 Using the matrix() Function:** The matrix() function is the most common way to create a matrix in R. It allows you to specify the number of rows and columns and optionally fill the matrix by rows.

**Basic Syntax:**
matrix(data, nrow, ncol, byrow = FALSE, dimnames = NULL)

**1. data**: The data to be filled in the matrix.
**2. nrow**: Number of rows.
**3. ncol**: Number of columns.
**4. byrow**: Logical value indicating whether to fill the matrix by rows (default is `FALSE`).
**5. dimnames**: Optional list of row and column names.

**Example (Basic Matrix)**

```
mat <- matrix(1:9, nrow = 3, ncol = 3)
```

```
print(mat)
```

**Output:**

```
     [,1] [,2] [,3]
[1,]    1    4    7
[2,]    2    5    8
[3,]    3    6    9
```

**6.1.2 Combining Vectors using rbind() and cbind():** You can create matrices by combining vectors as rows or columns using the rbind() and cbind() functions.

**Example (Using rbind() to Combine Vectors as Rows)**

```
row1 <- c (1, 2, 3)
row2 <- c (4, 5, 6)
row3 <- c (7, 8, 9)
mat_rbind <- rbind(row1, row2, row3)   <- Combining vectors as row
print(mat_rbind)
```

**Output:**

```
     [,1] [,2] [,3]
Row1    1    4    7
Row2    2    5    8
Row3    3    6    9
```

**Example (Using cbind() to Combine Vectors as Columns)**

```
col1 <- c(1, 4, 7)
col2 <- c(2, 5, 8)
col3 <- c(3, 6, 9)
mat_cbind <- cbind(col1, col2, col3)   <- Combining vectors as column
print(mat_cbind)
```

**Output:**

```
     col1 col2 col3
[1,]    1    2    3
[2,]    4    5    6
[3,]    7    8    9
```

**6.1.3 Converting Data Frames to Matrices:** Data frames can be converted to matrices using the as.matrix() function. This is useful when you have tabular data in a data frame and need to perform matrix operations.

**Example: Converting a Data Frame to a Matrix**

```
df <- data.frame(A = 1:3, B = 4:6, C = 7:9)     ← Creating a data frame
print(df)
Output:
  A B C
1 1 4 7
2 2 5 8
3 3 6 9

mat_from_df <- as.matrix(df)                    ← Converting the data frame to a matrix
print(mat_from_df)
Output:
     A B C
[1,] 1 4 7
[2,] 2 5 8
[3,] 3 6 9
```

**6.1.4 Creating Diagonal Matrices:** Diagonal matrices have non-zero elements only on the diagonal, from the top-left to the bottom-right.

**Example (Creating a Diagonal Matrix using diag())**

```
diag_mat <- diag(c(1, 2, 3))     ← Creating a diagonal matrix
print(diag_mat)

Output:
     [,1] [,2] [,3]
[1,]    1    0    0
[2,]    0    2    0
[3,]    0    0    3
```

**6.1.5 Creating Identity Matrices:** Identity matrices are square matrices with ones on the diagonal and zeros elsewhere.

**Example (Creating an Identity Matrix using diag())**

```
identity_mat <- diag(4)
print(identity_mat)

Output:
     [,1] [,2] [,3] [,4]
[1,]    1    0    0    0
[2,]    0    1    0    0
[3,]    0    0    1    0
[4,]    0    0    0    1
```

**6.1.6. Creating Matrices from Vectors Using dim():** You can also convert a vector into a matrix by setting its dimensions using the dim() function.

**Example (Converting a Vector to a Matrix)**

```
vec <- 1:9                  ← Creating a vector

dim(vec) <- c (3, 3)        ← Setting dimensions to convert it into a 3x3 matrix
print(vec)

Output:
     [,1] [,2] [,3]
[1,]    1    4    7
[2,]    2    5    8
[3,]    3    6    9
```

## 6.2 Accessing Matrix Elements

Accessing elements within a matrix in R is a fundamental operation for data manipulation and analysis. Here's a comprehensive guide on how to access and manipulate matrix elements using various methods:

### 6.2.1 Basic Access

**1. Single Element Access:** Elements in a matrix can be accessed using their row and column indices. The general syntax is matrix[row, column].

```
mat <- matrix(1:9, nrow = 3, ncol = 3)
element <- mat[2, 3]     # Accesses the element in the 2nd row and 3rd column
print(element)

Output: 8
```

**2. Entire Row or Column:** To access an entire row or column, you can leave the other index blank.

```
row <- mat [2,]          # Accesses the entire 2nd row
print(row)

column <- mat[, 3]       # Accesses the entire 3rd row
print(column)

Output:
2 5 8
7 8 9
```

**3. Submatrix Access:** You can access a submatrix by specifying ranges for the row and column indices.

```
submatrix <- mat[1:2, 2:3]   # Accesses the submatrix consisting of rows 1-2 and columns
print(submatrix)

Output:
     [,1] [,2]
[1,]   4    5
[2,]   7    8
```

### 6.2.2 Advanced Access Methods

**1. Using Logical Indexing:** Logical indexing allows you to select elements based on condition

```
selection <- mat[mat > 5]    # Selects elements greater than 5
print(selection)

Output:
6 7 8 9
```

**2. Accessing Elements by Names:** You can assign names to the rows and columns of a matrix and then access elements using these names.

```
dimnames(mat) <- list (c("row1", "row2", "row3"),
c("col1", "col2", "col3"))
element <- mat["row2", "col3"]
print(element)

Output:
8
```

**3. Accessing Multiple Elements by Indices:** You can access multiple elements by providing vectors of row and column indices.

```
elements <- mat[c(1, 3), c(1, 2)]
print(elements)

Output:
     [,1] [,2]
[1,]    1    4
[2,]    3    6
```

Accesses elements at (1,1), (1,2), (3,1), and (3,2)

**4. Combining Indices with cbind():** Use cbind() to combine row and column indices for more specific selections.

```
elements <- mat[cbind(c(1, 2, 3), c(3, 2, 1))]
print(elements)

Output:
7 5 3
```

### 6.2.3 Modifying Matrix Elements

**1. Updating Single Elements:** You can update a single element by specifying its row and column indices.

```
mat[2, 3] <- 10
print(mat)

Output:
     [,1] [,2] [,3]
[1,]    1    2    3
[2,]    4    5   10
[3,]    7    8    9
```

Updates the element in the 2nd row and 3rd column to 10

**2. Updating Rows and Columns:** Entire rows or columns can be updated by specifying the row or column index and assigning new values.

```
mat[1, ] <- c(10, 11, 12)
print(mat)

Output:
     [,1] [,2] [,3]
[1,]   10   11   12
[2,]    4    5   10
[3,]    7    8    9
```

Updates the entire 1st row

```
mat[2, ] <- c(20, 21, 22)
print(mat)

Output:
     [,1] [,2] [,3]
[1,]   10   20   12
[2,]    4   21   10
[3,]    7   22    9
```

**3. Updating Submatrices:** Submatrices can be updated by specifying ranges for rows and columns and assigning a new matrix of appropriate dimensions.

```
mat[1:2, 2:3] <- matrix(c(30, 31, 32, 33), nrow = 2)
print(mat)
```

**Output:**

```
     [,1] [,2] [,3]
[1,]   10   30   32
[2,]    4   31   33
[3,]    7   22    9
```

**6.2.4 Special Considerations**

**1. Handling Out-of-Bounds Indices:** Accessing out-of-bounds indices will result in NA.

```
out_of_bounds <- mat[4, 4]
print(out_of_bounds)
```

**Output:**

```
NA
```

**2. Using drop Argument:** By default, R drops dimensions when accessing a single row or column. Use the drop = FALSE argument to retain the matrix structure.

```
single_row <- mat[1, , drop = FALSE]
print(single_row)
```

**Output:**

```
     [,1] [,2] [,3]
[1,]   10   30   32
```

```
single_column <- mat[, 1, drop = FALSE]
print(single_column)
```

**Output:**

```
     [,1]
[1,]   10
[2,]    4
[3,]    7
```

**3. Logical Matrix for Subsetting:** Use a logical matrix to subset elements that meet certain conditions.

```
logical_matrix <- matrix(c(TRUE, FALSE, TRUE, FALSE, TRUE, FALSE, TRUE, FALSE,
TRUE), nrow = 3)
subset_elements <- mat[logical_matrix]
print(subset_elements)
```

**Output:**

```
1 3 31 32 9
```

**6.3 Matrix Arithmetic and Manipulation in R**

Matrices in R support a variety of arithmetic operations and manipulations that allow for sophisticated data analysis and computations. This section provides a detailed guide on how to perform these operations, with examples to illustrate each concept.

**6.3.1 Element-wise Operations:** Element-wise operations are performed on corresponding elements of matrices of the same dimension.

1. Addition:

```
mat1 <- matrix(1:9, nrow = 3)
mat2 <- matrix(9:1, nrow = 3)

mat_add <- mat1 + mat2
print(mat_add)
```

**Output:**

```
     [,1] [,2] [,3]
[1,]   10   10   10
[2,]   10   10   10
[3,]   10   10   10
```

2. Subtraction:

```
mat_sub <- mat1 - mat2
print(mat_sub)
```

**Output:**

```
     [,1] [,2] [,3]
[1,]   -8   -2    4
[2,]   -6    0    6
[3,]   -4    2    8
```

3. Multiplication:

```
mat_mult <- mat1 * mat2
print(mat_mult)
```

**Output:**

```
     [,1] [,2] [,3]
[1,]    9   24   21
[2,]   16   25   16
[3,]   21   24    9
```

4. Division:

```
mat_div <- mat1 / mat2
print(mat_div)
```

**Output:**

```
          [,1]      [,2]     [,3]
[1,] 0.1111111 0.6666667 2.333333
[2,] 0.2500000 1.0000000 4.000000
[3,] 0.4285714 1.5000000 9.000000
```

**6.3.2 Scalar Operations:** Scalar operations involve performing arithmetic operations between a matrix and a single number (scalar). These operations are also element-wise.

1. Scalar Addition:

```
scalar_add <- mat1 + 10
print(scalar_add)
```

**Output:**

```
     [,1] [,2] [,3]
[1,]   11   14   17
[2,]   12   15   18
[3,]   13   16   19
```

2. Scalar Multiplication:

```
scalar_mult <- mat1 * 2
print(scalar_mult)
```

**Output:**

```
     [,1] [,2] [,3]
[1,]    2    8   14
[2,]    4   10   16
[3,]    6   12   18
```

**6.3.3 Matrix Multiplication:** Matrix multiplication (dot product) is different from element-wise multiplication and is performed using the %*% operator.

```
mat1 <- matrix(1:4, nrow = 2)
mat2 <- matrix(5:8, nrow = 2)

mat_mult_dot <- mat1 %*% mat2
print(mat_mult_dot)
```

**Output:**

```
     [,1] [,2]
[1,]   23   31
[2,]   34   46
```

**6.3.4 Transposing a Matrix:** Transposing a matrix flips it over its diagonal, switching rows with columns. This is done using the t() function.

```
mat_transpose <- t(mat1)
print(mat_transpose)
```

**Output:**

```
     [,1] [,2]
[1,]    1    2
[2,]    3    4
```

**6.3.5 Applying Functions to Matrices:** You can apply functions to rows or columns of a matrix using the apply() function.

1. Sum of Rows:

```
row_sums <- apply(mat1, 1, sum)     ← Sum of each row
print(row_sums)

Output: 4 6
```

2. Mean of Columns:

```
col_means <- apply(mat1, 2, mean)   ← Mean of each column
print(col_means)

Output: 1.5 3.5
```

#### 6.3.6 Matrix Manipulation

**1. Reshaping a Matrix:** Reshaping involves changing the dimensions of a matrix without changing its data.

```
col_means <- apply(mat1, 2, mean)   ← Mean of each column
print(col_means)

Output: 1.5 3.5
```

**2. Binding Rows and Columns:** You can bind matrices or vectors as rows or columns using rbind() and cbind().

```
mat3 <- matrix(1:6, nrow = 2, ncol = 3)
mat4 <- matrix(7:12, nrow = 2, ncol = 3)

mat_rbind <- rbind(mat3, mat4)
print(mat_rbind)

mat_cbind <- cbind(mat3, mat4)
print(mat_cbind)
```

**Output 1 :**

```
     [,1] [,2] [,3]
[1,]    1    3    5
[2,]    2    4    6
[3,]    7    9   11
[4,]    8   10   12
```

**Output 2:**

```
     [,1] [,2] [,3] [,4] [,5] [,6]
[1,]    1    3    5    7    9   11
[2,]    2    4    6    8   10   12
```

**3. Dimension Manipulation:** You can change the dimensions of a matrix using the dim() function.

```
dim(mat3) <- c(3, 2)
print(mat3)
```

**Output:**

```
     [,1] [,2]
[1,]    1    4
[2,]    2    5
[3,]    3    6
```

### 6.4 Matrix Operations in R in Detail

Matrix operations in R are essential for various mathematical computations and data analyses. Here, we cover a range of matrix operations, including basic arithmetic, matrix multiplication, transposition, and advanced operations such as calculating the determinant, inverse, eigenvalues, and more.

#### 6.4.1 Matrix Operations

**1. Basic Arithmetic Operations**

**- Addition and Subtraction:** Matrices of the same dimensions can be added or subtracted element-wise.

```
mat1 <- matrix(1:9, nrow = 3)
mat2 <- matrix(9:1, nrow = 3)

mat_add <- mat1 + mat2
```

```
print(mat_add)

mat_sub <- mat1 - mat2
print(mat_sub)
```

**Output 1:**

```
     [,1] [,2] [,3]
[1,]   10   10   10
[2,]   10   10   10
[3,]   10   10   10
```

**Output 2:**

```
     [,1] [,2] [,3]
[1,]   -8   -2    4
[2,]   -6    0    6
[3,]   -4    2    8
```

- **Multiplication and Division:** Element-wise multiplication and division are performed using * and /.

```
mat_mult <- mat1 * mat2        ← Element-wise multiplication
print(mat_mult)

mat_div <- mat1 / mat2         ← Element-wise division
print(mat_div)
```

**Output 1:**

```
     [,1] [,2] [,3]
[1,]    9   24   21
[2,]   16   25   16
[3,]   21   24    9
```

**Output 2:**

```
          [,1]      [,2]     [,3]
[1,] 0.1111111 0.6666667 2.333333
[2,] 0.2500000 1.0000000 4.000000
[3,] 0.4285714 1.5000000 9.000000
```

- **Matrix Multiplication:** Use the %*% operator for matrix multiplication.

```
mat3 <- matrix(1:4, nrow = 2)
mat4 <- matrix(4:1, nrow = 2)

mat_mult2 <- mat3 %*% mat4     ← Matrix multiplication
print(mat_mult2)
```

**Output 1:**

```
     [,1] [,2]
[1,]   13    5
[2,]   20    8
```

**2. Transposition:** Transpose a matrix using the t() function, which switches the rows and columns.

```
mat_transpose <- t(mat1)
print(mat_transpose)
```

**Output 1:**

```
     [,1] [,2] [,3]
[1,]    1    2    3
[2,]    4    5    6
[3,]    7    8    9
```

**3. Determinant:** Calculate the determinant of a square matrix using the det() function.

```
det_mat <- det(mat1)
print(det_mat)
```

**Output 1:** 0

**4. Inverse:** Calculate the inverse of a square, non-singular matrix using the solve() function.

```
inv_mat <- matrix(c(2, 3, 1, 4), nrow = 2)
inv_result <- solve(inv_mat)
print(inv_result)
```

**Output 1:** 0

**5. Eigenvalues and Eigenvectors:** Compute the eigenvalues and eigenvectors of a square matrix using the eigen() function.

```
eig_result <- eigen(mat1)
print(eig_result$values) # Eigenvalues      <-- Eigenvalues
print(eig_result$vectors) # Eigenvectors    <-- Eigenvectors
```

**Output 1:**
```
1.611684e+01 -1.116844e+00 -5.700691e-16
```

**Output 2:**
```
          [,1]       [,2]       [,3]
[1,] -0.4645473 -0.8829060  0.4082483
[2,] -0.5707955 -0.2395204 -0.8164966
[3,] -0.6770438  0.4038651  0.4082483
```

**6. Matrix Rank:** Determine the rank of a matrix using the qr() function.

```
rank_mat <- qr(mat1)$rank
print(rank_mat)
```

**Output:** 2

**7. Cross Product and Outer Product**

**- Cross Product:** Compute the cross product of two matrices using the crossprod() function.

```
cross_prod <- crossprod(mat1)
print(cross_prod)

Output:
     [,1] [,2] [,3]
[1,]   14   32   50
[2,]   32   77  122
[3,]   50  122  194
```

- **Outer Product:** Compute the outer product of two vectors using the outer() function.

```
vec1 <- c(1, 2, 3)
vec2 <- c(4, 5, 6)
outer_prod <- outer(vec1, vec2)
print(outer_prod)

Output:
     [,1] [,2] [,3]
[1,]    4    5    6
[2,]    8   10   12
[3,]   12   15   18
```

**8. Solving Linear Systems:** Solve linear systems of equations using the solve() function.

```
A <- matrix(c(2, 1, 1, 3), nrow = 2)    <-- Solving a linear system Ax = b
b <- c(1, 2)
x <- solve(A, b)
print(x)    <-- Solution vector x

Output:
     [,1] [,2] [,3]
[1,]    4    5    6
[2,]    8   10   12
[3,]   12   15   18
```

**9. Singular Value Decomposition (SVD):** Perform SVD using the svd() function, which decomposes a matrix into its singular values and vectors.

```
svd_result <- svd(mat1)
print(svd_result$u)    <-- Left singular vectors

Output 2:
           [,1]        [,2]       [,3]
[1,] -0.4796712  0.77669099  0.4082483
[2,] -0.5723678  0.07568647 -0.8164966
[3,] -0.6650644 -0.62531805  0.4082483

print(svd_result$d)    <-- Singular values
```

```
Output 2:
1.684810e+01 1.068370e+00 5.039188e-17

print(svd_result$v)                    <-- Right Singular vectors

Output 3:
        [,1]      [,2]      [,3]
[1,] -0.2148372 -0.8872307 -0.4082483
[2,] -0.5205874 -0.2496440  0.8164966
[3,] -0.8263375  0.3879428 -0.4082483
```

**10. Matrix Exponentiation:** Raise a matrix to a power using the expm package (needs to be installed and loaded).

```
install.packages("expm")               <-- Matrix exponentiation
library(expm)
mat_power <- mat1 %^% 2
print(mat_power)
print(svd_result$v)

Output 3:
  [,1] [,2] [,3]
[1,]  30  66 102
[2,]  36  81 126
[3,]  42  96 150
```

**11. Diagonal Extraction and Creation**

**- Extracting Diagonal Elements:** Extract the diagonal elements using the diag() function.

```
diag_elements <- diag(mat1)
print(diag_elements)
```

**Output 3:** 1 5 9

**- Creating a Diagonal Matrix:** Create a diagonal matrix from a vector using the diag() function.

```
vec <- c(1, 2, 3)
diag_mat <- diag(vec)
print(diag_mat)
```

**Output 3:**

```
     [,1] [,2] [,3]
[1,]   1    0    0
[2,]   0    2    0
[3,]   0    0    3
```

**Summary**
- **Matrix:** A two-dimensional, homogeneous data structure with elements arranged in rows and columns.
- **Homogeneous:** All elements must be of the same type.
- **Column-Major Order:** Elements are filled column-wise by default.
- **matrix() Function:** Creates a matrix by specifying data, rows, and columns.

- **rbind() Function:** Combines vectors as rows to create a matrix.
- **cbind() Function:** Combines vectors as columns to create a matrix.
- **Diagonal Matrix:** A matrix with non-zero elements only on the diagonal.
- **Identity Matrix:** A square matrix with ones on the diagonal and zeros elsewhere.
- **Element-wise Operations:** Operations performed on corresponding elements of matrices.
- **Scalar Operations:** Arithmetic operations between a matrix and a single number.

**Glossary**

- **Inverse:** A matrix that, when multiplied by the original, results in an identity matrix using solve().
- **Eigenvalues and Eigenvectors:** Values and vectors describing the variance in the data using eigen().
- **Matrix Rank:** Dimension of the vector space generated by the matrix rows or columns using qr().
- **Cross Product:** Binary operation on two matrices resulting in another matrix using crossprod().
- **Outer Product:** Binary operation on two vectors resulting in a matrix using outer().
- **Singular Value Decomposition (SVD):** Factorization of a matrix into singular values and vectors using svd().
- **Diagonal Extraction and Creation:** Operations to extract or create diagonal elements in matrices using diag().

# Exercise

**Exercise 1 – Multiple choice questions**

1. What does the byrow argument in the matrix() function specify?
   a) The number of rows b) The number of columns
   c) Whether to fill the matrix by rows d) The data type of the elements
2. How do you access the element in the second row and third column of a matrix named mat?
   a) mat[3, 2] b) mat[2, 3] c) mat(2, 3) d) mat[3][2]

**Exercise 2 – Fill in the blanks**

1. The function used to create an identity matrix in R is __________.
2. To access an entire row or column in a matrix, you can leave the __________ blank in the index.

**Exercise 3 – True or False**

1. Matrices in R can contain elements of different data types.
2. The diag() function can be used to extract diagonal elements from a matrix.

**Exercise 4 – Short question answers**

1. Explain the difference between element-wise multiplication and matrix multiplication in R, providing examples for each.
2. How can you access a submatrix from a larger matrix in R? Provide an example.

**Exercise 5 – Long question answers**

1. Discuss the various methods to create matrices in R, including using the matrix() function, combining vectors with rbind() and cbind(), converting data frames, and creating diagonal and identity matrices. Provide examples for each method.
2. Describe the process of accessing and modifying matrix elements in R, including single elements, entire rows and columns, submatrices, and using logical indexing. Provide examples to illustrate each method.

# Answers

**Exercise 1** – 1. c) 2. b)
**Exercise 2** – 1. diag() 2. index
**Exercise 3** – 1. False 2. True

## Online Resources

**Practice Paper**
**Link:** https://forms.gle/9c1ujqS5QJ8ZF9Lh6
**QR Code**

**Project Video**
**Link:** https://www.youtube.com/playlist?list=PLzlh_31VWEFohu3FSOtULTK3HT8DZMDM4
**QR Code**

**YouTube Video Playlist Link**
**Link**
https://www.youtube.com/playlist?list=PLzlh_31VWEFohu3FSOtULTK3HT8DZMDM4
**QR Code**

**Test Paper**
**Chapter-6**
**Matrix**

**Time Duration: 40 Minutes** **Maximum**
**Marks: 25**

**General Instructions:**
1. The question paper consists of 12 questions and is divided into four sections, A, B, C and D.
2. All questions are compulsory.
3. Section A comprises MCQs, Fill in the blanks and True or False carrying one marks each.
4. Section B comprises VSAQs(very short answers questions) carrying two marks each.
5. Section C comprises SAQs(short questions) carrying four marks each.
6. Section D comprises long questions carrying five marks each.

## SECTION-A

**I. Multiple choice questions:** **(1*2=2)**

1. Which function is used to transpose a matrix in R?
   a) transpose() b) invert()
   c) solve() d) t()
2. Which operator is used for matrix multiplication in R?
   a) * b) /
   c) %*% d) ^

**II. Fill in the blanks:** **(1*2=2)**

1. The __________ function is used to calculate the determinant of a matrix.
2. The function __________ is used to compute the eigenvalues and eigenvectors of a matrix.

**III. True or False:** **(1*2=2)**

1. The rbind() function combines vectors as columns to form a matrix.
2. The t() function transposes a matrix by switching its rows and columns.

## SECTION-B

**IV. Very Short answers type questions-I** **(2*3=6)**

1. How do you create a 3x3 matrix in R filled by rows using the matrix() function
2. What function is used to bind vectors as columns in R?
3. Which function would you use to compute the cross product of two matrices?

## SECTION-C

**V. Short answers type questions-II** **(4*2=8)**

1. Describe the process of transposing a matrix and provide an example using the t() function.
2. What are the steps to calculate the inverse of a square matrix in R? Provide an example using the solve() function.

## SECTION-D

**VI. Long answers type questions** **(5*1=5)**

1. Explain advanced matrix operations in R, such as calculating the determinant, inverse, eigenvalues, and eigenvectors, performing matrix exponentiation, and solving linear systems. Provide detailed examples for each operation.

# Chapter 7:Strings

**In this chapter you will learn about:**
**- Strings in R**
**- Creating Strings**
**- Basic Strings Operations**
**- Advance String Operations**
**- String Manipulation Functions**
**- Strings Handling Packages**

**Strings in R**

Strings in R are sequences of characters used to represent text. They are a fundamental data type in R and are often used to store and manipulate textual data. Strings can be created using quotes (either single or double) and can contain letters, numbers, symbols, and spaces. Here are some key aspects of strings in R:

**Key Characteristics of Strings in R**

- **Character Data Type:** Strings in R are represented as character data type. Each element of a character vector is a string.
- **Flexibility:** Strings can contain a mix of letters, numbers, and special characters. They can be of any length.
- **String Operations:** R provides a variety of functions for string manipulation, including concatenation, splitting, formatting, and more.
- **Storage in Vectors:** Strings are often stored in character vectors, where each element is a string.

## 7.1 Creating Strings

Strings in R are sequences of characters used to represent text data. Creating and manipulating strings is a fundamental aspect of data analysis and programming in R. Below, we discuss various methods to create strings in R.

**7.1.1 Basic String Creation:** Strings can be created using either single quotes (') or double quotes (").

- Using Double Quotes:

```
string <- "Hello, World!"
print(string)

Output: "Hello, World!"
```

Creating a string using double quotes

- Using Single Quotes:

```
string <- 'Hello, R!'
print(string)

Output: 'Hello, R!'
```

Creating a string using single quotes

**Creating Strings with Variables:** Strings can be stored in variables, which allows for easier manipulation and combination with other strings or variables.

- Concatenating Strings with Variables:

```
name <- "Alice"
greeting <- paste("Hello,", name)
print(greeting)

Output: "Hello, Alice!"
```

Storing strings in variable
Concatenate strings

- **Using sprintf() for String Formatting:** The sprintf() function allows for formatted string creation, similar to printf in C.

```
age <- 30
string <- sprintf("My name is %s and I am %d years old.", name, age)
print(string)

Output: "My name is Alice and I am 30 years old."
```

Creating formatted strings

**7.1.3 Creating Multi-Line Strings:** Multi-line strings can be created using the cat() function or by using newline characters (\n).

- Using cat() Function:

```
cat("This is a multi-line string.\nIt has multiple lines.")

Output:
This is a multi-line string.
It has multiple lines.
```

Creating a multi-line string

- Using Newline Characters:

```
string <- "This is a multi-line string.\nIt has multiple lines."
print(string)

Output:
"This is a multi-line string.\nIt has multiple lines."
```

Creating a multi-line string using newline characters

**7.1.4 Creating Strings with Special Characters:** Special characters in strings can be represented using escape sequences.

- Escape Sequences:

**1.** **\n** for newline
**2.** **\t** for tab
**3.** \\ for backslash
**4.** **\"** for double quote
**5.** **\'** for single quote

```
string <- "This is a string with a newline character.\nAnd a
tab character:\tEnd of string."
print(string)

Output:
"This is a string with a newline character.\nAnd a tab
character:\tEnd of string."
```

Using escape sequences in strings

**7.1.5 Creating Strings from Other Data Types:** Strings can also be created from other data types using the as.character() function.

- Converting Numbers to Strings:

```
num <- 123
string <- as.character(num)     ← Converting a number to a string
print(string)

Output: 123
```

- Converting Logical Values to Strings:

```
value <- TRUE
string <- as.character(value)
print(string)
```

**Output:** "TRUE"

**7.1.6 Creating Vectors of Strings:** Vectors of strings can be created using the c() function.

- Creating a Vector of Strings:

```
fruits <- c("apple", "banana", "cherry")
print(fruits)
```

**Output:** : "apple" "banana" "cherry"

**7.1.7 paste() and paste0():** The paste() and paste0() functions are used to concatenate strings in R.

**- Using paste():** The paste() function concatenates strings with a space or specified separator.

```
str1 <- "Hello"
str2 <- "World"
combined <- paste(str1, str2)
print(combined)
```

**Output:** : "Hello World"

```
combined_sep <- paste(str1, str2, sep = ", ")
print(combined_sep)
```

**Output:** "Hello, World"

**- Using paste0():** The paste0() function concatenates strings without any separator.

```
combined_no_sep <- paste0(str1, str2)
print(combined_no_sep)
```

**Output:** "HelloWorld"

**7.2 Basic String Operations**

**7.2.1 Concatenation:** Use the paste() or paste0() function to concatenate strings.

```
str2 <- "World"
concatenated_str <- paste(str1, str2)       # Adds a space by default
concatenated_str0 <- paste0(str1, str2)     # No space added
print(concatenated_str)
print(concatenated_str0)

Output: "Hello World"
"HelloWorld
```

**7.2.2 String Length:** Use the nchar() function to get the length of a string.

```
str_length <- nchar("Hello, World!")
print(str_length)
```

**Output:** 13

**7.2.3 Substring:** Use the substr() function to extract or replace substrings.

```
str <- "Hello, World!"
substring <- substr(str, 1, 5)      # Extracts "Hello"
print(substring)

substr(str, 8, 12) <- "Earth"       # Replaces "World" with "Earth"
print(str)  # "Hello, Earth!"

Output: 13
```

**7.2.4 Changing Case:** Use toupper() and tolower() to change the case of strings.

```
upper_str <- toupper("Hello, World!")
lower_str <- tolower("Hello, World!")
print(upper_str)
```

**Output:** "HELLO, WORLD!"

```
print(lower_str)
```

**Output:** "hello, world!"

### 7.3 Advanced String Operations

**7.3.1 Regular Expressions:** Using regex for pattern matching and text manipulation.
**Functions:** grep(), grepl(), regexpr(), gregexpr(), regmatches().

```
upper_str <- toupper("Hello, World!")
lower_str <- tolower("Hello, World!")
print(upper_str)
```

**Output:** "HELLO, WORLD!"

```
print(lower_str)
```

**Output:** "hello, world!"

**7.3.2 String Matching and Searching:** Finding patterns within strings.

```
upper_str <- toupper("Hello, World!")
lower_str <- tolower("Hello, World!")
print(upper_str)
```

**Output:** "HELLO, WORLD!"

```
print(lower_str)
```
**Output:** "hello, world!"

**7.3.3 Advanced Formatting:** Using format() for advanced string formatting.

```
formatted_str <- format(123.456, nsmall = 2)
```

**7.3.4 String Distance:** Calculating the distance between strings using adist().

```
distance <- adist("kitten", "sitting")
```

**7.4 String Manipulation Functions**

**7.4.1 Trimming and Padding:**
- Removing whitespace using trimws().
- Padding strings using str_pad() from the stringr package.

```
trimmed_str <- trimws("  Hello  ")
library(stringr)
padded_str <- str_pad("Hello", width = 10, side = "both")
```

**Output:** "Hello"

**7.4.2 Substring Extraction:** Extracting substrings using substring() and substr().

```
sub_str <- substring("Hello, World!", 8, 12)
```

**Output:** "World"

**7.4.3 Splitting Strings:** Splitting strings into components using strsplit().

```
split_str <- strsplit("apple,banana,cherry", split = ",")
```

**Output:** "apple"  "banana" "cherry"

**7.4.4 Replacing Substrings:** Replacing parts of a string using sub() and gsub().

```
replaced_str <- sub("World", "R", "Hello, World!")
global_replaced_str <- gsub("o", "0", "Hello, World!")
print(replaced_str)
print(global_replaced_str)
```

**Output:** "Hello R!"
"Hell0 World!"

**7.5 String Handling Packages**
R provides several powerful packages for handling and manipulating strings. These packages offer a wide range of functions for tasks such as pattern matching, string replacement, extraction, concatenation, and more. Below are some of the most commonly used string handling packages in R, along with examples to illustrate their usage.

**7.5.1 Base R:** R's base functions for string handling include nchar(), substr(), and others.

- **nchar():** Returns the number of characters in a string.

```
nchar("Hello, World!")
```

**Output:** 13

- **substr():** Extracts or replaces substrings in a character vector.

```
substr("Hello, World!", 1, 5)
```

**Output:** "Hello"

**7.5.2 Stringr:** The stringr package provides a set of consistent, easy-to-use functions for string handling.

- **str_length():** Returns the number of characters in a string.

```
library(stringr)
str_length("Hello, World!")
```

**Output:** 13

- **str_sub():** Extracts substrings.

```
str_sub("Hello, World!", 1, 5)
```

**Output:** "Hello"

- **str_detect():** Detects the presence of a pattern in a string.

```
str_detect("Hello, World!", "World")
```

**Output:** TRUE

- **str_replace():** Replaces the first occurrence of a pattern in a string.

```
str_replace("Hello, World!", "World", "R")
```

**Output:** "Hello, R!"

- **str_replace_all():** Replaces all occurrences of a pattern in a string.

```
str_replace_all("Hello, World! World!", "World", "R")
```

**Output:** "Hello, R! R!"

**7.5.3. stringi:** The stringi package offers comprehensive string handling capabilities, including locale-aware operations.

- **stri_length():** Returns the number of characters in a string.

```
library(stringi)
stri_length("Hello, World!")
```

**Output:** 13

- **stri_sub():** Extracts substrings.

```
stri_sub("Hello, World!", 1, 5)
```

**Output:** "Hello"

- **stri_detect_regex():** Detects the presence of a pattern in a string.

```
stri_detect_regex("Hello, World!", "World")
```

**Output:** TRUE

- **stri_replace_all_regex():** Replaces all occurrences of a pattern in a string.

```
stri_replace_all_regex("Hello, World! World!", "World", "R")
```

**Output:** "Hello, R! R!"

**7.5.4. lubridate:** Although primarily used for date-time manipulation, lubridate can be useful for handling strings related to dates and times.
- **parse_date_time():** Parses a character vector into a date-time object.

```
library(lubridate)
parse_date_time("2023-07-26 12:34:56", "ymd HMS")
```

**Output:** "2023-07-26 12:34:56 UTC"

- **ymd():** Converts a string in year-month-day format to a date object.

```
ymd("2023-07-26")
```

**Output:** "2023-07-26"

**7.5.5. glue:** The glue package is used for string interpolation, which allows embedding R expressions inside strings.

- **glue():** Embeds R expressions inside a string.

```
library(glue)
name <- "World"
glue("Hello, {name}!")
```

**Output:** "Hello, World!"

- **glue_data():** Uses data from a list or data frame to embed in strings.

```
data <- list(name = "World")
glue_data(data, "Hello, {name}!")
```

**Output:** "Hello, World!"

**7.5.6. tm:** The tm package is widely used in text mining and provides functions for text preprocessing.

- **Corpus():** Creates a text corpus.

```
library(tm)
docs <- Corpus(VectorSource(c("Hello, World!", "Text mining in R.")))
```

- **tm_map():** Applies transformations to text data.

```
docs <- tm_map(docs, content_transformer(tolower))
```

**Summary**
- **Character Data Type**: Strings in R are represented as character data type, stored in character vectors.
- **String Creation**: Strings can be created using single or double quotes and stored in variables.
- **Special Characters**: Special characters in strings are represented using escape sequences (\n for newline, \t for tab, etc.).
- **Concatenation**: Strings can be concatenated using paste() and paste0().
- **String Length**: The length of a string can be determined using the nchar() function.
- **Substring Extraction**: Use substr() and substring() to extract or replace parts of strings.
- **Changing Case**: Convert strings to uppercase or lowercase using toupper() and tolower().

**Glossary**
- **Multi-Line Strings**: Create multi-line strings using cat() or newline characters (\n).
- **String Formatting**: Use sprintf() for formatted string creation.
- **Advanced String Operations**: Utilize regular expressions with functions like grep(), grepl(), regexpr(), gregexpr(), and regmatches() for pattern matching and text manipulation.
- **Trimming and Padding**: Use trimws() to remove whitespace.
- **String Splitting**: Split strings into components using strsplit().
- **String Replacement**: Replace parts of strings using sub() and gsub().

# Exercise

**Exercise 1 – Multiple choice questions**
1. Which function in R is used to create a string?
a. as.numeric()
b. as.character()
c. as.logical()
d. as.factor()

2. Which function concatenates strings without any separator in R?
a. paste()
b. paste0()
c. sprintf()
d. cat()

**Exercise 2 – Fill in the blanks**
1. The function used to create formatted strings in R, similar to printf in C, is __________.
2. Strings in R are often stored in __________ vectors.

**Exercise 3 – True or False**
1. The function used to create formatted strings in R, similar to printf in C, is __________.
2. Strings in R are often stored in __________ vectors.

**Exercise 4 – Short question answers**
1. Explain the difference between paste() and paste0() functions in R with examples.
2. Describe how to use the substr() function to extract a substring from the 3rd to the 5th character in a string.

**Exercise 5 – Long question answers**
1. Discuss the various methods to create strings in R, including basic string creation, creating strings with variables, multi-line strings, and special characters. Provide examples for each method.

2. Describe the different string manipulation functions available in the stringr package. Provide examples of how to use str_length(), str_sub(), str_detect(), and str_replace_all().

## Answers

**Exercise 1** – 1. b) 2. b)
**Exercise 2** – 1. sprintf() 2. character
**Exercise 3** – 1. True 2. False

**Online Resources**

**Practice Paper**
**Link:** https://forms.gle/sFC3mkumuqtHzXLt7
**QR Code**

**Project Video**
**Link:** https://www.youtube.com/playlist?list=PLzlh_31VWEFrAujKi1tG2DEqZBVWihQvQ
**QR Code**

**YouTube Video Playlist Link**

**Link**
https://www.youtube.com/playlist?list=PLzlh_31VWEFrAujKi1tG2DEqZBVWihQvQ
**QR Code**

**Test Paper**
**Chapter-7**
**Strings**

**Time Duration: 40 Minutes** **Maximum Marks: 25**

**General Instructions:**
1. The question paper consists of 12 questions and is divided into four sections, A, B, C and D.
2. All questions are compulsory.
3. Section A comprises MCQs, Fill in the blanks and True or False carrying one marks each.
4. Section B comprises VSAQs(very short answers questions) carrying two marks each.

5. Section C comprises SAQs(short questions) carrying four marks each.
6. Section D comprises long questions carrying five marks each.

## SECTION-A

**I. Multiple choice questions:** **(1*2=2)**

1. What does the nchar() function do in R?
a. Concatenates strings
b. Extracts substrings
c. Calculates the length of a string
d. Splits a string

2. Which package provides the str_length() function?
a. stringr
b. lubridate
c. tm
d. glue

**II. Fill in the blanks:** **(1*2=2)**

1. To remove whitespace from the beginning and end of a string, use the __________ function.
2. The __________ function from the stringi package replaces all occurrences of a pattern in a string.

**III. True or False:** **(1*2=2)**

1. The substr() function in R can be used to extract and replace substrings.
2. The str_detect() function from the stringr package is used to detect the presence of a pattern in a string.

## SECTION-B

**IV. Very Short answers type questions-I** **(2*3=6)**

1. How do you create a string with the text "Hello, World!" in R?
2. Which function would you use to concatenate the strings "data" and "science" without any separator?
3. What function from the stringr package returns the number of characters in a string?

## SECTION-C

**V. Short answers type questions-II** **(4*2=8)**

1. What are escape sequences in strings? Provide examples of at least two escape sequences.
2. How can you convert a numeric vector to a character vector in R? Provide an example.

## SECTION-D

**VI. Long answers type questions** **(5*1=5)**

1. Explain how to use regular expressions in R for pattern matching and text manipulation. Include examples using grep(), grepl(), regexpr(), gregexpr(), and regmatches().

# Chapter 8: Arrays

**In this chapter you will learn about:**
- Creating Arrays
- Access Array Elements
- Modifying Array Elements
- Array Manipulations
- Array Operations
- Array Functions
- Array Applications

**Arrays in R**
Arrays are multi-dimensional data structures that can hold elements of the same type. Arrays extend the concept of vectors and matrices to more than two dimensions. They are particularly useful for representing multi-dimensional data and performing complex data manipulations.

**Key Characteristics of Arrays in R**
- **Homogeneous Data Type:** All elements in an array must be of the same type (e.g., numeric, character, or logical).
- **Multi-dimensional Structure:** Arrays can have more than two dimensions, making them more versatile than matrices.
- **Dimension Names:** Arrays can have names assigned to their dimensions for easier access and interpretation.
- **Array Operations:** R provides various functions for creating, accessing, manipulating, and performing operations on arrays.
- **Flexible Size:** The size of each dimension can be specified when creating the array.

## 8.1 Creating Arrays

### 8.1.1 Using the array() Function

The array() function is the primary way to create arrays in R. It takes a vector of elements and converts it into an array with specified dimensions.

- Basic Syntax:

```
array(data = NA, dim = length(data),
dimnames = NULL)
```

- Arguments:
- **data:** The data to be filled in the array.
- **dim:** A vector indicating the dimensions of the array.
- **dimnames:** An optional list of dimension names.

- Example: Basic Array Creation

```
arr <- array(1:18, dim = c(3, 3, 2))
print(arr)
```

**Output:**

```
, , 1
     [,1] [,2] [,3]
[1,]   1    4    7
[2,]   2    5    8
[3,]   3    6    9

, , 2
     [,1] [,2] [,3]
[1,]  10   13   16
[2,]  11   14   17
[3,]  12   15   18
```

**8.1.2. Creating Arrays from Vectors:** You can create arrays by converting vectors and specifying the desired dimensions.

```
vec <- 1:24
arr <- array(vec, dim = c(2, 3, 4))
print(arr)
```

Creating a 2

**Output:**

```
, , 1
     [,1] [,2] [,3]
[1,]   1    3    5
[2,]   2    4    6

, , 2
     [,1] [,2] [,3]
[1,]   7    9   11
[2,]   8   10   12

, , 3
     [,1] [,2] [,3]
[1,]  13   15   17
[2,]  14   16   18

, , 4
     [,1] [,2] [,3]
[1,]  19   21   23
[2,]  20   22   24
```

**8.1.3. Naming Dimensions:** You can name the dimensions of an array to make the data more interpretable.

```
dim_names <- list(
  c("Row1", "Row2"),
  c("Col1", "Col2", "Col3"),
  c("Layer1", "Layer2")
)
arr <- array(1:12, dim = c(2, 3, 2),
dimnames = dim_names)
print(arr)
```

**Output:**

```
, , Layer1
     Col1 Col2 Col3
Row1   1   3   5
Row2   2   4   6

, , Layer2
     Col1 Col2 Col3
Row1   7   9  11
Row2   8  10  12
```

**4. Creating Multi-Dimensional Arrays:** Arrays can have more than three dimensions. You can specify the dime

```
arr <- array(1:24, dim = c(2, 2, 2, 3))
print(arr)
```

**Output:**

```
, , 1, 1
     [,1] [,2]
[1,]    1    3
[2,]    2    4

, , 2, 1
     [,1] [,2]
[1,]    5    7
[2,]    6    8

, , 1, 2
     [,1] [,2]
[1,]    9   11
[2,]   10   12

, , 2, 2
     [,1] [,2]
[1,]   13   15
[2,]   14   16

, , 1, 3
     [,1] [,2]
[1,]   17   19
[2,]   18   20

, , 2, 3
     [,1] [,2]
[1,]   21   23
[2,]   22   24
```

**8.1.5. Initializing Arrays with Specific Values:** You can initialize an array with specific values by passing a vector of those values to the data argument.

```
arr <- array(0, dim = c(2, 3))
print(arr)
```

**Output:**

```
     [,1] [,2] [,3]
[1,]    0    0    0
[2,]    0    0    0
```

**8.1.6. Using dim() to Convert Vectors to Arrays:** You can also use the dim() function to set the dimensions of a vector, effectively converting it into an array.

```
vec <- 1:12
dim(vec) <- c(3, 4)
print(vec)
```

**Output:**

```
     [,1] [,2] [,3] [,4]
[1,]    1    4    7   10
[2,]    2    5    8   11
[3,]    3    6    9   12
```

**8.2 Accessing Array Elements**

Accessing elements in an array is similar to accessing elements in matrices but extends to multiple dimensions. Here are various ways to access elements:

**8.2.1. Single Element Access:** To access a single element, specify the indices for each dimension.

```
array <- array(1:18, dim = c(3, 3, 2))
element <- array[2, 3, 1]
print(element)
```

Accessi

**Output:** 8

**8.2.2 Accessing Entire Dimension:** You can access all elements along a specific dimension by leaving other indices blank.

```
row <- array[2, , 1]
print(row)
```

Accessi

**Output:** 2 5 8

```
column <- array[, 1,]
print(column)
```

Accessi

**Output:**

```
     [,1] [,2]
[1,]    1   10
[2,]    2   11
[3,]    3   12
```

**8.2.3 Accessing Subarrays:** You can access subarrays by specifying ranges for indices.

```
subarray <- array[1:2, 1:2, 1]
print(subarray)
```

Accessing

**Output:**

```
     [,1] [,2]
[1,]    1    4
[2,]    2    5
```

**8.2.4 Using Logical Indexing:** Logical vectors can be used to access elements that meet certain conditions.

```
greater_than <- array[array > 10]
print(greater_than)
```

**Output:**
11 12 13 14 15 16 17 18

**8.2.5 Using Named Dimensions:** Arrays can have named dimensions, allowing for more intuitive access.

```
dimnames(array) <- list(Row = c("A", "B", "C"), Col
c("X", "Y", "Z"), Layer = c("L1", "L2"))
element <- array["B", "Y", "L1"]
print(element)
```

**Output:** 5

**8.2.6 Combining Indices with c():** You can combine indices using c() to access elements.

```
indices <- array[c(1, 3), c(2, 3), 1]
print(indices)
```

**Output:**

```
    col
Row y z
  A 4 7
  C 6 9
```

**8.3 Modifying Array Elements**

**8.3.1 Modifying Single Elements:** To modify a single element in an array, use the indexing syntax to specify the position of the element and assign a new value.

```
array[1, 2, 2] <- 99
print(array)
```

**Output:**

```
, , Layer = L1          , , Layer = L2
  col                     col
Row x y z               Row x y z
 A 1 4 7                 A 10 99 16
 B 2 5 8                 B 11 14 17
 C 3 6 9                 C 12 15 18
```

**8.3.2 Modifying Multiple Elements:** You can modify multiple elements in an array by specifying a range of indices or using logical indexing.

**- Using Index Ranges:** You can specify ranges for indices to modify multiple elements at once.

```
array[1, , 1] <- c(10, 20, 30)
print(array)
```

**Output:**

```
, , Layer = L1          , , Layer = L2
  col                     col
Row x y z               Row x y z
 A 10 20 30              A 10 99 16
 B 2 5 8                 B 11 14 17
 C 3 6 9                 C 12 15 18
```

**- Using Logical Indexing:** Logical conditions can be used to identify and modify elements that meet certain criteria.

```
array[array > 10] <- 0
print(array)
```

**Output:**

```
, , Layer = L1          , , Layer = L2
  col                     col
Row x y z               Row x y z
 A 10 0 0                A 10 0 0
 B 2 5 8                 B 0 0 0
 C 3 6 9                 C 0 0 0
```

**8.3.3 Modifying Entire Rows, Columns, or Layers:** You can also modify entire rows, columns, or layers of an array.

**- Modifying Rows:** Specify the row index and leave the column and layer indices blank to modify an entire row.

```
array[2, , 1] <- c(100, 200, 300)
print(array)
```

Modifying the second row of the first layer

**Output:**

```
, , Layer = L1
   col
Row  x   y   z
 A  10   0   0
 B 100 200 300
 C   3   6   9

, , Layer = L2
   col
Row x y z
 A 10 0 0
 B 0 0 0
 C 0 0 0
```

- **Modifying Columns:** Specify the column index and leave the row and layer indices blank to modify an entire column.

```
array[, 3, 2] <- c(50, 60, 70)
print(array)
```

**Output:**

```
, , Layer = L1
   col
Row  x   y   z
 A  10   0   0
 B 100 200 300
 C   3   6   9

, , Layer = L2
   col
Row x y z
 A 10 0 50
 B 0 0 60
 C 0 0 70
```

- **Modifying Layers:** Specify the layer index and leave the row and column indices blank to modify an entire layer.

```
array[,, 1] <- array[,, 1] * 2
print(array)
```

**Output:**

```
, , Layer = L1
   col
Row  x   y   z
 A  20   0   0
 B 200 400 600
 C   6  12  18

, , Layer = L2
   col
Row x y z
 A 10 0 50
 B 0 0 60
 C 0 0 70
```

**8.4 Using Functions to Modify Array Elements:** R provides various functions that can be applied to modify array elements.

**8.4.1 Using apply():** The apply () function can be used to apply a function to margins of an array, such as rows, columns, or layers.

```
array_modified<- apply(array, c(3), function(x) x + 5)
print(array_modified)
```

**Output:**

```
  Layer
     L1 L2
[1,] 25 15
[2,] 205 5
[3,] 11 5
[4,] 5 5
[5,] 405 5
[6,] 17 5
[7,] 5 55
[8,] 605 65
[9,] 23 75
```

**8.4.2 Using lapply() and sapply():** These functions can be used to apply a function to each element or sub-array.

```
array_list <- as.list(array)
array_list_mod <- lapply(array_list,
function(x) x + 5)
print(array_list_mod)
```

**Output:**
25 205 11 5 405 17 5 605 23 15 5 5 5 5 5 55 65 75

**8.5 Manipulating Arrays:** Arrays can be manipulated in various ways, including modifying elements, reshaping, and combining arrays.

**8.5.1 Modifying Elements:**

```
array[1, 1, 1] <- 100
print(array)
```

Modify... positio...

**Output:**

```
, , Layer = L1
   col
Row  x   y   z
 A 100   0   0
 B 200 400 600
 C   6  12  18

, , Layer = L2
   col
Row x y z
 A 10 0 50
 B 0 0 60
 C 0 0 70
```

**8.5.2 Reshaping Arrays:** You can change the dimensions of an array using the dim() function.

```
dim(array) <- c(9, 2)
print(array)
```

**Output:**

```
     [,1] [,2]
 [1,] 100   10
 [2,] 200    0
 [3,]   6    0
 [4,]   0    0
 [5,] 400    0
 [6,]  12    0
 [7,]   0   50
 [8,] 600   60
 [9,]  18   70
```

**8.5.3 Combining Arrays:** Combine arrays using functions like abind() from the abind package.

```
install.packages("abind")
library(abind)

array1 <- array(1:12, dim = c(3, 2, 2))
array2 <- array(13:24, dim = c(3, 2, 2))
combined_array <- abind(array1, array2, along = 3)
print(combined_array)
```

**Output:**

```
, , 1
     [,1] [,2]
[1,]    1    4
[2,]    2    5
[3,]    3    6

, , 2
     [,1] [,2]
[1,]    7   10
[2,]    8   11
[3,]    9   12

, , 3
     [,1] [,2]
[1,]   13   16
[2,]   14   17
[3,]   15   18

, , 4
     [,1] [,2]
[1,]   19   22
[2,]   20   23
[3,]   21   24
```

**8.5.4 Splitting Arrays:** Arrays can be split into subarrays using indexing or custom functions.

```
array_split <- split(array, f = array[, , 1])
print(array_split)
```

**Output:**
1 13 2 14 3 15 4 16 5 17 6 18 7 19 8 20 9 21 10 22 11 23 12 24

**8.6 Array Operations**

**8.6.1 Element-wise Operations:** Arrays support element-wise operations similar to matrices and vectors. These operations are applied element-by-element across the entire array.

- Addition:

```
array1 <- array(1:8, dim = c(2, 2, 2))
array2 <- array(8:1, dim = c(2, 2, 2))
array_add <- array1 + array2
print(array_add)
```

**Output:**

```
, , 1
     [,1] [,2]
[1,]    9    9
[2,]    9    9

, , 2
     [,1] [,2]
[1,]    9    9
[2,]    9    9
```

- Subtraction:

```
array_sub <- array1 - array2
print(array_sub)
```

**Output:**

```
, , 1
     [,1] [,2]
[1,]   -7   -3
[2,]   -5   -1

, , 2
     [,1] [,2]
[1,]    1    5
[2,]    3    7
```

- Multiplication:

```
array_mult <- array1 * array2
print(array_mult)
```

**Output:**

```
, , 1
     [,1] [,2]
[1,]    8   18
[2,]   14   20

, , 2
     [,1] [,2]
[1,]   20   14
[2,]   18    8
```

- Division:

```
array_div <- array1 / array2
print(array_div)
```

**Output:**

```
, , 1
```

```
          [,1]      [,2]
[1,] 0.1250000  0.5
[2,] 0.2857143  0.8

, , 2
     [,1]  [,2]
[1,] 1.25  3.5
[2,] 2.00  8.0
```

**8.6.2 Applying Functions Across Margins:** You can apply functions across specific dimensions (margins) of an array using the apply() function.

**- Summing Across Dimensions:**

```
sum_dim1 <- apply(array1, 1, sum)
print(sum_dim1)

Output: 16  20

sum_dim2 <- apply(array1, 2, sum)
print(sum_dim2)

Output:  14  22

sum_dim3 <- apply(array1, 3, sum)
print(sum_dim3)

Output: 10  26
```

**- Finding Mean Across Dimensions:**

```
mean_dim1 <- apply(array1, 1, mean)
print(mean_dim1)

Output: 4  5

mean_dim2 <- apply(array1, 2, mean)
print(mean_dim2)

Output:  3.5  5.5

mean_dim3 <- apply(array1, 3, mean)
print(mean_dim3)

Output: 2.5  6.5
```

**8.6.3 Transposing Arrays:** Transposing is typically associated with matrices, but you can also transpose multi-dimensional arrays by rearranging their dimensions using the aperm() function.

```
array1 <- array(1:8, dim = c(2, 2, 2))
transposed_array <- aperm(array1, c(2, 1, 3))
print(transposed_array)

Output:
, , 1
     [,1] [,2]
[1,]    1    2
[2,]    3    4

, , 2
     [,1] [,2]
[1,]    5    6
[2,]    7    8
```

**8.6.4 Reshaping Arrays:** You can change the dimensions of an array using the dim() function.

```
array1 <- array(1:12, dim = c(3, 2, 2))
print(array1)

Output:
, , 1                    , , 2
     [,1] [,2]                [,1] [,2]
[1,]    1    4           [1,]    7   10
[2,]    2    5           [2,]    8   11
[3,]    3    6           [3,]    9   12

dim(array1) <- c(2, 3, 2)
print(array1)

Output:
, , 1                          , , 2
     [,1] [,2] [,3]                 [,1] [,2] [,3]
[1,]    1    3    5            [1,]    7    9   11
[2,]    2    4    6            [2,]    8   10   12
```

Re

**8.7 Array Functions:**Functions can be applied to elements of arrays using apply() and other related functions.

**8.7.1 Using apply():** The apply() function applies a function along a specified margin of an array.

```
array_rows <- apply(array, c(1, 2), sum)
print(array_rows)

Output:
,      [,1] [,2] [,3] [,4]
[1,]   14   20   26   32
[2,]   16   22   28   34
[3,]   18   24   30   36
```

**8.7.2 Using lapply() and sapply():** These functions can be used to apply a function to each element of a list or vector, which can be useful with arrays.

```
array_list <- as.list(array)
array_lapply <- lapply(array_list, function(x) x^2)
print(array_lapply)

Output:
1 4 9 16 25 36 49 64 81 100 121 144 169 196 225 256
289 324 361 400 441 484 529 576

array_sapply <- sapply(array_list, function(x) x^2)
print(array_sapply)

Output:
1 4 9 16 25 36 49 64 81 100 121 144 169 196 225 256
289 324 361 400 441 484 529 576
```

**8.8 Array Applications**

- **Multidimensional Data Storage:** Arrays can store data in more than two dimensions, making them suitable for handling complex datasets, such as data collected over time or across different categories.
- **Mathematical and Statistical Computations:** Arrays are used for performing mathematical operations on multi-dimensional data, such as matrix operations, linear algebra computations, and statistical analysis.
- **Image Processing:** In image processing, arrays are used to represent images where each pixel value can be stored in a multi-dimensional array.
- **Time-Series Analysis:** Arrays can store time-series data, with dimensions representing time points and variables of interest, enabling efficient manipulation and analysis of temporal data.
- **Simulation and Modeling:** Arrays are used in simulations and modeling where data needs to be generated and stored across multiple dimensions for further analysis.

## Summary

- **Array:** A multi-dimensional data structure that stores elements of the same type across multiple dimensions.
- **Homogeneous Data Type:** Requirement that all elements in an array must be of the same type (e.g., numeric, character, logical).
- **Multi-dimensional Structure:** Arrays can have more than two dimensions, extending the capabilities of vectors and matrices.
- **Dimension Names:** Names assigned to the dimensions of an array to facilitate easier access and interpretation of data.
- **Element-wise Operations:** Operations applied to corresponding elements of arrays of the same dimension.
- **Simulation and Modeling:** Using arrays to store data generated from simulations or models across multiple dimensions for analysis.
- **Image Processing:** Using arrays to represent and manipulate images, where each pixel value is stored in a multi-dimensional array.

**Glossary**

- **apply():** A function used to apply another function to the margins of an array (e.g., rows, columns).
- **lapply():** A function that applies another function to each element of a list or vector, returning a list.
- **sapply():** A function similar to lapply(), but it attempts to simplify the result to a vector or matrix if possible.
- **dim():** A function used to get or set the dimensions of an array or matrix.
- **aperm():** A function used to transpose or permute the dimensions of an array.
- **abind():** A function from the abind package used to combine arrays along specified dimensions.
- **apply() function:** Applies a function to the rows, columns, or other margins of an array.
- **reshape:** Changing the dimensions of an array without changing its data.
- **Time-Series Analysis:** Storing and analyzing data collected over time using arrays, where dimensions represent time points and variables.

# Exercise

**Exercise 1 – Multiple choice questions**

**1.** Which function is primarily used to create an array in R?

a. matrix()
b. data.frame()
c. array()
d. c()

**2.** What does the `dim` argument in the `array()` function specify?

a. The data type of the elements
b. The dimensions of the array
c. The names of the dimensions
d. The length of the array

**Exercise 2 – Fill in the blanks**

1. Arrays in R can have names assigned to their dimensions using the __________ argument in the `array()` function.
2. The function __________ is used to apply a function across specific dimensions of an array.

**Exercise 3 – True or False**
1. Arrays in R can contain elements of different data types.
2. The `dim()` function can be used to set the dimensions of an array.

**Exercise 4 – Short question answers**
1. Explain how to access a single element in a three-dimensional array and provide an example.
2. Describe how to apply the `apply()` function to sum the elements across the first dimension of a 3D array.

**Exercise 5 – Long question answers**
1. Discuss the various methods to create arrays in R, including using the `array()` function, converting vectors, and naming dimensions. Provide examples for each method.
2. Describe the different ways to access and modify elements in an array, including single elements, entire dimensions, subarrays, and using logical indexing. Provide examples to illustrate each method.

## Answers

**Exercise 1** – 1. c) 2. b)
**Exercise 2** – 1. dimnames 2. apply()
**Exercise 3** – 1. False 2. True

**Online Resources**

**Practice Paper**
**Link** https://forms.gle/8uR5wPFZGDuEHrtq8
**QR Code**

**Project Video**
**Link:**
https://www.youtube.com/playlist?list=PLzlh_31VWEFrQ6O5XafGpfNYykxPgAUld
**QR Code**

**Youtube Video Playlist Link**
**Link:**https://www.youtube.com/playlist?list=PLzlh_31VWEFrQ6O5XafGpfNYykxPgAUld
**QR Code**

**Test Paper**

**Chapter-8**
**Arrays**

**Time Duration: 40 Minutes**
**Maximum Marks: 25**

**General Instructions:**
1. The question paper consists of 12 questions and is divided into four sections, A, B, C and D.
2. All questions are compulsory.
3. Section A comprises MCQs, Fill in the blanks and True or False carrying one marks each.
4. Section B comprises VSAQs(very short answers questions) carrying two marks each.
5. Section C comprises SAQs(short questions) carrying four marks each.
6. Section D comprises long questions carrying five marks each.

**SECTION-A**

**I. Multiple choice questions: (1*2=2)**
1. How can you name the dimensions of an array in R?
a. Using the names() function
b. Using the dimnames argument in the array() function
c. Using the rename() function
d. Using the names<- function

2. Which function can be used to apply a function to margins of an array?
a. lapply()
b. sapply()
c. apply()
d. mapply()

**II. Fill in the blanks: (1*2=2)**

1. To modify the dimensions of an array, you can use the __________ function.
2. The __________ function from the abind package is used to combine arrays.

**III. True or False: (1*2=2)**

1. The array() function can only create arrays with up to three dimensions.
2. You can use logical indexing to access elements in an array that meet certain conditions.

## SECTION-B

**IV. Very Short answers type questions-I (2*3=6)**

1. How do you create a 3x3x2 array in R using the array() function?
2. Which function would you use to apply a function to each margin of an array
3. How can you modify the dimensions of a vector to convert it into an array?

## SECTION-C

**V. Short answers type questions-II (4*2=8)**

1. What is the purpose of the dimnames argument in the array() function? Provide an example.
2. How can you combine two arrays using the abind() function? Provide an example.

## SECTION-D

**VI. Long answers type questions (5*1=5)**

1. Explain the array operations available in R, such as element-wise operations, applying functions across margins, transposing arrays, and reshaping arrays. Provide detailed examples for each operation.

# Chapter 9: Factors

**In this chapter you will learn about:**
- Creating Factors
- Accessing and Modifying Factors
- Factor Operations
- Factors in Data Frames
- Factors Conversion
- Factors Applications

**Factors**
Factors are a special data structure in R used for categorical data. They are particularly useful for representing and managing data that has a fixed number of unique values, known as levels. Factors are widely used in statistical modeling and data analysis as they help in handling and analyzing categorical data efficiently.

**Key Characteristics of Factors in R**
- **Categorical Data Representation:** Factors are used to represent categorical data, which can be either nominal (unordered categories) or ordinal (ordered categories).
- **Levels:** Factors have levels, which are the unique values that a factor can take. These levels can be ordered or unordered.
- **Efficient Storage:** Factors store data more efficiently than character vectors, especially when there are many repeated values.
- **Statistical Modeling:** Factors are essential for statistical modeling as they help in managing categorical predictors.

## 9.1 Creating Factors

**9.1.1 Using the factor() Function:** The factor() function is the primary way to create factors in R. It converts a vector into a factor.
**Basic Syntax:**

```
factor(x, levels = unique(x), labels = levels, ordered = FALSE)
```

**Arguments:**
- **x:** The input vector to be converted into a factor.
- **levels:** The unique values of the input vector. If not provided, they are inferred from x.
- **labels:** Optional labels for the levels
- **ordered:** Logical value indicating if the factor is ordered.

**Example: Basic Factor Creation**

```
colors <- c("red", "blue", "green", "blue", "red")
factor_colors <- factor(colors)
print(factor_colors)
```

**Output:** red  blue  green  blue  red
Levels: blue green red

**9.1.2 Specifying Levels and Labels:** You can explicitly specify the levels and labels when creating a factor.

```
sizes <- c("small", "large", "medium", "large", "small")
factor_sizes <- factor(sizes, levels = c("small", "medium", "large"))
print(factor_sizes)
```

**Output:** small  large  medium  large  small
Levels: small medium large

```
factor_sizes_labels <- factor(sizes, levels = c("small", "medium",
"large"), labels = c("S", "M", "L"))
print(factor_sizes_labels)

Output: S L M L S
Levels: S M L
```

Creating a factor with specified lables

**9.1.3 Creating Ordered Factors:** Ordered factors represent ordinal data, where the order of levels matters.

```
education <- c("highschool", "bachelor", "master", "bachelor", "phd")
factor_education <- factor(education, levels = c("highschool", "bachelor",
"master", "phd"), ordered = TRUE)
print(factor_education)

Output: highschool  bachelor  master   bachelor  phd
Levels: highschool < bachelor < master < phd
```

Creating an ordered factor

**9.1.4 Converting Existing Variables to Factors:** You can convert existing variables to factors using the as.factor() function.

```
numbers <- c(1, 2, 3, 2, 1)
factor_numbers <- as.factor(numbers)
print(factor_numbers)

Output: 1 2 3 2 1
Levels: 1 2 3
```

Converting a numeric vector to a factor

**9.2 Accessing and Modifying Elements of Factors**

**9.2.1 Accessing Elements of Factors:** Factors can be accessed in a similar manner to vectors.

```
data <- c("low", "medium", "high", "medium", "low")
factor_data <- factor(data, levels = c("low", "medium", "high"))
```

- Accessing Single Element:

```
element <- factor_data[2]
print(element)

Output: medium
```

Access the second element

- Accessing Multiple Elements:

```
elements <- factor_data[c(1, 3)]
print(elements)

Output: low high
```

Access the first and third element

- Using Logical Indexing:

```
medium_elements <- factor_data[factor_data == "medium"]
print(medium_elements)

Output: medium medium
```

Access elements that are "medium"

- Using Factor Levels:

```
levels(factor_data)

Output: "low"   "medium"   "high"
```
← Access the levels of the factor

**9.2.2 Modifying Factors:** Factors can be modified in terms of their levels and the values they contain.

**- Changing Levels:** You can rename the levels of a factor using the levels() function.

```
levels(factor_data) <- c ("Low", "Medium", "High")
print(factor_data)
Output: Low   Medium High   Medium Low
```
← Rename levels

**- Adding Levels:** To add new levels to a factor, you can use the levels() function to set the levels explicitly.

```
levels(factor_data) <- c(levels(factor_data), "Very High")
print(levels(factor_data))
Output: "Low"    "Medium"   "High"    "Very High"
```

**- Reordering Levels:** The factor() function can be used to reorder levels.

```
levels(factor_data) <- c(levels(factor_data), "Very High")
print(levels(factor_data))
Output: "Low"    "Medium"   "High"    "Very High"
```

**- Dropping Unused Levels:** The droplevels() function removes levels that are not used in the data.

```
factor_data <- factor(factor_data)
factor_data <- droplevels(factor_data)
print(levels(factor_data))

Output: "High"  "Medium"  "Low"
```

**- Changing Values:** You can change the values of a factor by assigning new values to specific elements.

```
factor_data[1] <- "High"
print(factor_data)

Output: High   Medium High   Medium Low
```

**- Combining Levels:** Sometimes, you may want to combine multiple levels into one.

```
levels(factor_data) <- c("High", "Medium", "Medium")
print(factor_data)

Output: High   Medium High   Medium Medium
```

**9.3 Factor Operations**

**9.3.1. Tabulating Factors:** Use the table() function to create a frequency table of the levels in a factor.

```
factor_colors <- factor(c("red", "green", "blue", "green", "red", "blue", "blue"))
color_table <- table(factor_colors)
print(color_table)
```

Creating a factor

Creating a frequency table

**Output:** factor_colors

```
blue green  red
  3    2    2
```

**9.3.2 Merging Factors:** Combine two factors using the c() function, ensuring they have the same levels.

```
factor1 <- factor(c("a", "b", "c"))
factor2 <- factor(c("b", "c", "a"))
merged_factor <- factor(c(as.character(factor1), as.character(factor2)), levels = c("a", "b", "c"))
print(merged_factor)
```

**Output:** a b c b c a

Levels: a b c

**9.3.3 Reordering Factor Levels:** Reorder factor levels using the factor() function with the levels argument.

```
reordered_sizes <- fact or(ordered_sizes, levels = c("large", "medium", "small"))
print(reordered_sizes)
```

**Output:** medium small large small medium

Levels: large < medium < small

**9.3.4 Renaming Factor Levels:** Rename factor levels using the levels() function.

```
levels(factor_colors) <- c("Dark Red", "Light Green", "Sky Blue")
print(factor_colors)
```

**Output:** Sky Blue Light Green Dark Red Light Green Sky Blue Dark Red Dark Red

Levels: Dark Red Light Green Sky Blue

### 9.4 Factors in Data Frames

**9.4.1 Creating a Data Frame with Factors:**

```
data <- data.frame(
  Name = c("Alice", "Bob", "Carol", "David"),
  Gender = factor(c("Female", "Male", "Female", "Male")),
  Age = c(25, 30, 22, 35)
)
print(data)
```

**Output:**

```
   Name Gender Age
1 Alice Female  25
2   Bob   Male  30
3 Carol Female  22
4 David   Male  35
```

**9.4.2 Checking the Structure:**

```
str(data)
```

**Output:**

```
'data.frame':    4 obs. of 3 variables:
$ Name  : chr  "Alice" "Bob" "Carol" "David"
$ Gender: Factor w/ 2 levels "Female","Male": 1 2 1 2
$ Age   : num  25 30 22 35
```

**9.4.3 Accessing and Modifying Factor Levels:**

```
levels(data$Gender)                    <- Accessing levels

Output: "Female" "Male"

levels(data$Gender) <- c("F", "M")     <- Modifying levels
print(data)
Output:
  Name Gender Age
1 Alice    F   25
2   Bob    M   30
3 Carol    F   22
4 David    M   35
```

**9.5 Factors Conversion**
**9.5.1 Converting Character Vectors to Factors**

```
char_vector <- c("apple", "banana", "cherry", "apple", "cherry")
factor_vector <- as.factor(char_vector)
print(factor_vector)
```

**Output:**
apple banana cherry apple cherry
Levels: apple banana cherry

**9.5.2 Converting Factors to Character Vectors**

```
factor_vector <- factor(c("apple", "banana", "cherry"))
char_vector <- as.character(factor_vector)      <- Using as.character()
print(char_vector)

Output: "apple" "banana" "cherry"
```

Converts each level of the factor to its corresponding character string.

**9.5.3 Converting Factors to Numeric Vectors**
**- Converting Factor Levels to Numeric Values**:

```
factor_vector <- factor(c("low", "medium", "high"), levels = c("low", "medium", "high"))
numeric_vector <- as.numeric(factor_vector)
print(numeric_vector)
```

**Output:** 1 2 3

This converts the factor to its underlying integer codes. Note that the numeric representation corresponds to the factor levels' order, not their original numeric values.
**- Converting Factor Labels to Numeric Values**:

```
factor_vector <- factor(c("1", "2", "3", "2", "1"))
numeric_vector <- as.numeric(as.character(factor_vector))
print(numeric_vector)
```

**Output:** 1 2 3 2 1

**9.5.4 Handling NA Values During Conversion**

- Including NA Levels:

```
char_vector <- c("apple", "banana", NA, "cherry", "apple")
factor_vector <- factor(char_vector, exclude = NULL)
print(factor_vector)
```

**Output:** apple banana <NA> cherry apple
Levels: apple banana cherry <NA>

By setting exclude = NULL, NA is treated as a valid factor level.

- Handling Missing Data:

```
factor_vector <- factor(c("low", "medium", NA, "high"))
factor_vector[is.na(factor_vector)] <- "medium"
print(factor_vector)
```

**Output:** low medium medium high
Levels: high low medium

This assigns a specific level to NA values.

**9.6 Factors Applications**

**1. Data Analysis and Visualization**
- **Categorical Data Representation:** Factors allow the representation of categorical data, making it easier to perform operations on such data, such as survey responses (Yes, No, Maybe).
- **Data Grouping:** Factors enable the grouping of data for analysis, such as grouping sales data by region or income levels ("Low", "Medium", "High").

**2. Plotting and Visualization:**
- **Bar Plots:** Factors facilitate the creation of bar plots to visualize the frequency of different categories.
- **Box Plots:** Factors allow the comparison of distributions across categories.

**3. Statistical Modeling**
- **Regression Analysis:** Factors are used in regression models to represent categorical independent variables, such as including a factor for gender in a regression model.
- **ANOVA (Analysis of Variance):** Factors are crucial in ANOVA for comparing means across different groups.

**4. Data Transformation**
- **Recode Factors:** Factors enable the transformation of factor levels to simplify analysis or visualization, such as recoding levels of a factor variable.
- **Reorder Levels:** Factors allow the reordering of levels based on specific criteria, such as frequency or another variable.

**5. Memory Efficiency**
- **Efficient Storage:** Factors are more memory-efficient for storing categorical data compared to character vectors. This is particularly useful when dealing with large datasets.

**6. Data Cleaning and Preprocessing**
- **Handling Missing Data:** Factors provide a structured way to manage and impute missing data, such as assigning a specific level to NA values.

**7. Machine Learning**
- **Feature Engineering:** Factors are used to encode categorical variables for machine learning models, such as encoding categorical variables for a decision tree model.

**8. Survey Analysis**
- **Survey Data:** Factors are ideal for handling survey data with predefined response options, making it easier to analyze survey responses.

**Summary**
- **Factor:** A data structure for categorical data in R.
- **Categorical Data:** Data that can be divided into groups or categories.
- **Levels:** Unique values that a factor can take.
- **Nominal Data:** Categorical data without an inherent order.
- **Ordinal Data:** Categorical data with a meaningful order.
- **factor() Function:** Function to create a factor from a vector.
- **as.factor() Function:** Function to convert an existing variable to a factor.
- **levels() Function:** Function to get or set the levels of a factor.
- **droplevels() Function:** Function to drop unused levels from a factor.
- **table() Function:** Function to create a frequency table of a factor's levels.

**Glossary**
- **c() Function**: Function to combine factors.
- **Recode**: Changing the levels of a factor for simplified analysis.
- **Reorder Levels**: Changing the order of levels in a factor.
- **Efficient Storage**: Saving memory by using factors instead of character vectors.
- **Handling NA**: Managing missing values in factors.
- **Feature Engineering**: Preparing factors for use in machine learning models.
- **Survey Analysis**: Using factors to analyze survey data with predefined responses.
- **Regression Analysis**: Using factors in regression models to handle categorical variables.
- **ANOVA (Analysis of Variance)**: Using factors to compare means across groups in ANOVA.

## Exercise

**Exercise 1 – Multiple choice questions**
**1.** Which function is primarily used to create factors in R?
**a.** as.factor()
**b.** factor()
**c.** levels()
**d.** ordered()

**2.** What argument in the factor() function specifies the unique values of the input vector?
**a.** labels
**b.** ordered
**c.** levels
**d.** x

**Exercise 2 – Fill in the blanks**
1. Factors are used for representing ________ data in R.
2. The ________ function is used to create ordered factors.

**Exercise 3 – True or False**
1. Factors can only represent ordinal data.
2. Using factors is more memory-efficient than using character vectors.

**Exercise 4 – Short question answers**
1. Explain the difference between nominal and ordinal data.
2. Why are factors more memory-efficient than character vectors?

**Exercise 5 – Long question answers**
1. Discuss the importance of factors in statistical modeling.
2. Explain the process of converting factors to numeric vectors and the potential pitfalls.

# Answers

**Exercise 1** – 1. c) 2. b)
**Exercise 2** – 1. categorical 2. ordered
**Exercise 3** – 1. False 2. True

### Online Resources

**Practice Paper**
**Link:** https://forms.gle/q2PJx435XdGkTpYu7
**QR Code**

**Project Video**

**Link:** https://www.youtube.com/playlist?list=PLzlh_31VWEFqovzf2UzHSiL3b6U2ygyuw
**QR Code**

### YouTube Video Playlist Link

**Link**
https://www.youtube.com/playlist?list=PLzlh_31VWEFqovzf2UzHSiL3b6U2ygyuw
**QR Code**

**Test Paper**

**Chapter-9**
**Factors**

**Time Duration: 40 Minutes** **Maximum**
**Marks: 25**

**General Instructions:**
1. The question paper consists of 12 questions and is divided into four sections, A, B, C and D.
2. All questions are compulsory.
3. Section A comprises MCQs, Fill in the blanks and True or False carrying one marks each.
4. Section B comprises VSAQs(very short answers questions) carrying two marks each.
5. Section C comprises SAQs(short questions) carrying four marks each.
6. Section D comprises long questions carrying five marks each.

**SECTION-A**

**I. Multiple choice questions:** **(1*2=2)**
1. Which function converts an existing variable to a factor in R?
a. factor()
b. as.factor()
c. levels()
d. ordered()

2. Which function is used to rename the levels of a factor?
a. droplevels()
b. levels()
c. factor()
d. as.factor()

**II. Fill in the blanks:** **(1*2=2)**
1. The ________ function is used to create a frequency table of factor levels.
2. The ________ function removes levels that are not used in the data.

**III. True or False:** **(1*2=2)**
1. The factor() function cannot reorder the levels of a factor.
2. You can use the as.numeric() function to convert factor levels to their underlying integer codes..

**SECTION-B**

**IV. Very Short answers type questions-I** **(2*3=6)**
1. What is a factor in R?
2. Name two types of categorical data represented by factors.
3. What function is used to convert a character vector to a factor?

**SECTION-C**

**V. Short answers type questions-II** **(4*2=8)**
1. How do you handle missing data in factors?
2. Describe how to reorder levels of a factor.

**SECTION-D**

**VI. Long answers type questions** **(5*1=5)**
1. Describe the applications of factors in data visualization and how they enhance the process.

# Chapter 10: Data frames

**In this chapter you will learn about:**
- Creating Data Frames
- Access and Modify Data Frames
- Data Frame Operations
- Data Frame Functions
- Applying Functions to Data Frame
- Factors Applications

**Data Frame**
A data frame is a fundamental data structure in R, used for storing data tables. It is similar to a table in a database or an Excel spreadsheet, where data is organized in rows and columns. Each column in a data frame can contain data of different types (numeric, character, factor, etc.), making it a versatile structure for data analysis.

**Key Characteristics of a Data Frame:**
- **Tabular Structure**: Data frames are two-dimensional, meaning they have rows and columns.
- **Column Heterogeneity**: Columns can have different data types. For example, one column can contain numeric values, while another can contain character strings.
- **Row Homogeneity**: Each row in a data frame represents an observation and should contain data related to that observation.

**Advantages of Data Frame**
- **Versatility:** Handle different data types in columns.
- **Ease of Use:** Intuitive and similar to Excel or SQL tables.
- **Comprehensive Functionality:** Wide range of functions for data manipulation.
- **Integration:** Works seamlessly with many R functions and packages.
- **Data Cleaning:** Facilitates filtering, sorting, and modifying data.
- **Flexibility:** Easily import/export data from/to various formats.

**Disadvantages of Data Frame**
- **Memory Consumption:** Can be memory-intensive for large datasets.
- **Performance Limitations:** Less efficient for very large or complex operations.
- **Lack of Type Checking:** Columns can be coerced to unintended data types.
- **Limited for Non-Tabular Data:** Not suitable for hierarchical or multidimensional data.
- **Potential Inconsistencies:** Risk of misaligned rows/columns during manipulation.
- **Learning Curve:** Challenging for beginners to fully utilize.

## 10.1 Create Data Frame
Creating a data frame in R involves defining the data for each column and then combining these columns into a data frame. Here's a detailed step-by-step guide:

### 10.1.2 Step-by-Step Guide to Creating a Data Frame in R

**1. Load Required Packages (if any):**
You may need to install and load packages for additional functionalities, but basic data frame creation does not require any additional packages.

**2. Define the Data for Each Column:**
Create vectors for each column you want in your data frame. Each vector should contain data of the same type.

**Example:** Let's create a data frame with student information, including ID, Name, Age, Major, and Grade.

```
ID <- 1:5
Name <- c("Jay", "Riya", "Rahul", "Sachi", "Piyush")
```

```
Age <- c(20, 21, 19, 22, 20)
Major <- c("Math", "Science", "Engineering", "Arts", "Commerce")
Grade <- c("A", "B", "A", "C", "B")
```

**3. Combine Columns into a Data Frame:**

Use the data.frame() function to combine these vectors into a data frame.

```
students_df <- data.frame(
  ID = ID,
  Name = Name,
  Age = Age,
  Major = Major,
  Grade = Grade
)
```

**4. View and Verify the Data Frame:**

Print and summarize the data frame to ensure it has been created correctly.

```
print(students_df)                                    ← Print the data frame
Output:
  ID  Name  Age   Major    Grade
1 1   Jay   20    Math       A
2 2   Riya  21   Science     B
3 3  Rahul  19  Engineering  A
4 4  Sachi  22    Arts       C
5 5  Piyush 20  Commerce     B

str(students_df)                                      ← View the structure of the data frame
Output:
'data.frame': 5 obs. of 5 variables:
 $ ID   : int 1 2 3 4 5
 $ Name : chr "Jay" "Riya" "Rahul" "Sachi" ...
 $ Age  : num 20 21 19 22 20
 $ Major: chr "Math" "Science" "Engineering" "Arts" ...
 $ Grade: chr "A" "B" "A" "C" ...
```

```
summary(students_df)                                  ← Get summary statistics of the data frame
Output:
       ID      Name               Age          Major              Grade
 Min.   : 1   Length:5          Min.   :19.0   Length:5           Length:5
 1st Qu.: 2   Class :character  1st Qu.:20.0   Class :character   Class :character
 Median :3    Mode  :character  Median :20.0   Mode  :character   Mode  :character
 Mean   : 3                     Mean   :20.4
 3rd Qu.: 4                     3rd Qu.:21.0
 Max.   : 5                     Max.   :22.0
```

**10.2 Access and Modify Data Frame:** Accessing and modifying data frames in R involves various techniques for selecting, adding, and changing data within the data frame. Here's a detailed guide on how to perform these operations.

**10.2.1 Accessing Data in a Data Frame**

**1. Accessing Columns**

**- Using the $ Operator:**

```
names <- students_df$Name
```

```
print(names)
```

**Output:**
"Jay" "Riya" "Rahul" "Sachi" "Piyush"

- **Using Double Brackets [[ or Single Brackets [:**

```
names <- students_df[["Name"]]
print(names)
```

**Output:**
"Jay" "Riya" "Rahul" "Sachi" "Piyush"

```
names <- students_df["Name"]
print(names)
```

**Output:**
"Jay" "Riya" "Rahul" "Sachi" "Piyush"

**2. Accessing Rows**
- Using Row Indexing:

```
first_row <- students_df[1, ]        ← Access the first row
print(first_row)
```

**Output:**
```
  ID Name Age Major Grade
1  1  Jay  20  Math     A
```

```
first_two_rows <- students_df[1:2, ]        ← Access the multiple row
print(first_two_rows)
```

**Output:**
```
  ID Name Age   Major Grade
1  1  Jay  20    Math     A
2  2 Riya  21 Science     B
```

**3. Accessing Specific Elements**
- Using Row and Column Indexing:

```
element <- students_df[1, 2]        ← Access the element in the 1st row and 2nd column (Name of the first student)
print(element)
```

**Output:** "Jay"

**10.2.2 Modifying Data in a Data Frame**
1. Adding a New Column

```
students_df$Attendance <- c(90, 85, 88, 80, 95)
print(students_df)

Output:
  ID  Name Age   Major  Grade Attendance
1  1   Jay  20    Math     A        90
2  2  Riya  21  Science    B        85
3  3 Rahul  19 Engineering A        88
4  4 Sachi  22    Arts     C        80
5  5 Piyush 20 Commerce    B        95
```

Add a new column 'Attendance'

**2. Modifying Existing Columns**

- Changing Values in a Column:

```
students_df$Age[2] <- 22
print(students_df)

Output:
  ID  Name Age   Major  Grade Attendance
1  1   Jay  20    Math     A        90
2  2  Riya  22  Science    B        85
3  3 Rahul  19 Engineering A        88
4  4 Sachi  22    Arts     C        80
5  5 Piyush 20 Commerce    B        95
```

Change the 'Age' of the second student to 22

- Renaming Columns:

```
colnames(students_df)[colnames(students_df) == "Grade"] <- "FinalGrade"
print(students_df)
Output:
  ID  Name Age   Major   Final Grade Attendance
1  1   Jay  20    Math        A          90
2  2  Riya  22  Science       B          85
3  3 Rahul  19 Engineering    A          88
4  4 Sachi  22    Arts        C          80
5  5 Piyush 20 Commerce       B          95
```

Rename 'Grade' column to 'FinalGrade'

**3. Adding Rows**

- Using rbind() to Add a New Row:

```
new_student <- data.frame (
 ID = 6,
 Name = "Aman",
 Age = 23,
 Major = "Physics",
 FinalGrade = "A",
 Attendance = 92
)
students_df <- rbind(students_df, new_student)
print(students_df)

Output:
  ID  Name Age   Major   Final Grade Attendance
1  1   Jay  20    Math        A          90
2  2  Riya  22  Science       B          85
3  3 Rahul  19 Engineering    A          88
4  4 Sachi  22    Arts        C          80
5  5 Piyush 20 Commerce       B          95
6  6  Aman  23  Physics       A          92
```

Add a new row for a new student

**5. Removing Columns**

- Using NULL to Remove a Column:

```
students_df$Attendance <- NULL        # Remove the 'Attendance' column
print(students_df)

Output:
  ID  Name Age      Major  Final Grade
1  1   Jay  20       Math   A
2  2  Riya  22    Science   B
3  3 Rahul  19 Engineering  A
4  4 Sachi  22       Arts   C
5  5 Piyush 20   Commerce   B
6  6  Aman  23    Physics   A
```

**6. Removing Rows**

- Using Negative Indexing to Remove a Row:

```
students_df <- students_df[-2, ]      # Remove the 'Attendance' column
print(students_df)

Output:
  ID  Name Age      Major  Final Grade
1  1   Jay  20       Math   A
3  3 Rahul  19 Engineering  A
4  4 Sachi  22       Arts   C
5  5 Piyush 20   Commerce   B
6  6  Aman  23    Physics   A
```

**10.3 Data Frame Operations**

**10.3.1 Subsetting Data**

**- Select Specific Columns:**

```
subset_df <- students_df[, c("Name", "Age")]   # Select 'Name' and 'Age' columns
print(subset_df)

Output:
    Name  Age
1    Jay   20
3  Rahul   19
4  Sachi   22
5 Piyush   20
6   Aman   23
```

- Select Rows Based on Conditions:

```
grade_a_students <- subset(students_df, FinalGrade == "A")   # Select rows where 'FinalGrade' is 'A'
print(grade_a_students)

Output:
  ID  Name Age      Major  FinalGrade
1  1   Jay  20       Math   A
3  3 Rahul  19 Engineering  A
6  6  Aman  23    Physics   A
```

**10.3.2 Sorting Data**

- Using the order() Function:

```
sorted_df <- students_df[order(students_df$Age), ]
print(sorted_df)
Output:
  ID  Name Age      Major FinalGrade
3  3 Rahul  19 Engineering         A
1  1   Jay  20        Math         A
5  5 Piyush 20   Commerce          B
4  4 Sachi  22        Arts         C
6  6  Aman  23     Physics         A
```

Sort data frame by 'Age'

**10.3.3 Merging Data Frames**
**- Using merge() Function:**

```
attendance_df <- data.frame (
  ID = c(1, 2, 3, 4, 5, 6),
  Attendance = c(90, 85, 88, 80, 95, 92)
)
merged_df <- merge(students_df, attendance_df, by = "ID")
print(merged_df)

Output:

  ID  Name Age      Major FinalGrade Attendance
1  1   Jay  20        Math         A         90
2  3 Rahul  19 Engineering         A         88
3  4 Sachi  22        Arts         C         80
4  5 Piyush 20   Commerce          B         95
5  6  Aman  23     Physics         A         92
```

Create another data frame

Merge the two data frames

**10.3.4 Aggregating Data**
**- Using aggregate() Function:**

```
mean_age_by_major <- aggregate(Age ~ Major, data =
students_df, FUN = mean)
print(mean_age_by_major)

Output:
        Major Age
1        Arts  22
2    Commerce  20
3 Engineering  19
4        Math  20
5     Physics  23
```

Calculate the mean age of students by 'Major'

**10.4 Data Frame Conversion**

Data frame conversion refers to changing the data types of columns or transforming the entire data frame into another structure. This can be necessary for data analysis, ensuring compatibility with functions, or improving performance. Below are some common data frame conversion operations.

**1. Converting Column Data Types**

- Convert Column to Numeric

```
df <- data.frame (
ID = 1:5,
Age = c("20", "21", "19", "22", "20")
)
df$Age <- as.numeric(df$Age)
print(df)
```

Create a data frame

Convert 'Age' column to numeric

**Output:**

```
  ID Age
1  1  20
2  2  21
3  3  19
4  4  22
5  5  20
```

**- Convert Column to Character**

```
df$ID <- as.character(df$ID)
print(df)
```

Convert 'ID' column to character

**Output:**

```
  ID Age
1  1  20
2  2  21
3  3  19
4  4  22
5  5  20
```

**- Convert Column to Factor**

```
df$Age <- as.factor(df$Age)
print(df)
```

Convert 'Age' column to factor

**Output:**

```
  ID Age
1  1  20
2  2  21
3  3  19
4  4  22
5  5  20
```

**10.4.2 Converting Entire Data Frame to Matrix:** Converting a data frame to a matrix can be useful for certain mathematical operations.

```
matrix_df <- as.matrix(df)
print(matrix_df)
```

**Output:**

```
     ID  Age
[1,] "1" "20"
[2,] "2" "21"
[3,] "3" "19"
[4,] "4" "22"
```

```
[5,] "5" "20"
```

**10.4.2 Converting Entire Data Frame to List:** Sometimes, you may need to convert a data frame to a list for specific list-based operations.

```
list_df <- as.list(df)
print(list_df)
```

**Output:**

```
$ID
[1] "1" "2" "3" "4" "5"
$Age
[1] 20 21 19 22 20
Levels: 19 20 21 22
```

**10.4.3 Converting Data Frame to Tibble:** Tibbles are a modern take on data frames that are part of the tidyverse package. They provide a cleaner print method and better support for large data frames.

```
install.packages("tibble")
library(tibble)
```

← Install and load the tibble package

```
tibble_df <- as_tibble(df)
print(tibble_df)
```

← Convert the data frame to a tibble

**Output:**

```
# A tibble: 5 × 2
   ID   Age
 <chr> <fct>
1 1     20
2 2     21
3 3     19
4 4      22
5 5     20
```

**10.5 Applying Functions to Data Frames**

Applying functions to data frames is essential for data manipulation and analysis. You can apply functions to individual columns, rows, or the entire data frame using various R functions like apply, lapply, sapply, tapply, and mapply. Here's a detailed guide on how to apply these functions to data frames.

**10.5.1 apply Function:** The apply function is used to apply a function to the rows or columns of a matrix or data frame.

```
students_df <- data.frame(
  ID = 1:5,
  Age = c(20, 21, 19, 22, 20),
  Attendance = c(90, 85, 88, 80, 95)
)
```

← Create a data frame

```
column_sums <- apply(students_df[, -1], 2, sum)
print(column_sums)
```

← Apply the sum function to each column

**Output:**

```
Age Attendance
 102      438
```

```
row_sums <- apply(students_df[, -1], 1, sum)
print(row_sums)
```

← Apply the sum function to each row

**Output:**

```
110 106 107 102 115
```

**10.5.2 lapply Function:** The lapply function applies a function to each element of a list or data frame and returns a list.

```
column_means <- lapply(students_df[, -1], mean)
print(column_means)
```

Apply the mean function to each column (Excluding the ID column)

**Output:**

```
$Age
 20.4
$Attendance
 87.6
```

**10.5.3 sapply Function:** The sapply function is similar to lapply but tries to simplify the result to the most basic data structure possible.

```
column_means <- sapply(students_df[, -1], mean
print(column_means)
```

Apply the mean function to each column and simplify the result (Excluding the ID column)

**Output:**

```
$Age
 20.4
$Attendance
 87.6
```

**10.5.4 tapply Function:** The tapply function applies a function over subsets of a vector and is particularly useful for group-wise operations.

```
mean_age <- tapply(students_df$Attendance, students_df$Age, mean)
print(mean_age)
```

**Output:**

```
 19   20   21   22
88.0 92.5 85.0 80.0
```

**10.5.5 mapply Function:** The mapply function is a multivariate version of sapply. It applies a function to the corresponding elements of multiple arguments.

```
attendance_age_ratio <- function(attendance, age) {
  return(attendance / age)
}
ratios <- mapply(attendance_age_ratio, students_df$Attendance, students_df$Age)
print(ratios)
```

Create a custom function to calculate attendance to age ratio

Apply the custom function to 'Attendance' and 'Age'

**Output:**

```
 4.500000 4.047619 4.631579 3.636364 4.750000
```

**10.6 Applications of Data Frames**

**1. Data Analysis**

- **Descriptive Statistics:** Calculate summary statistics like mean, median, and standard deviation.
- **Data Cleaning:** Handle missing values and transform data for analysis.

**2. Data Visualization**

- **Creating Plots:** Use visualization libraries like ggplot2 to create various plots and charts.

**3. Machine Learning**
- **Model Training and Testing:** Store and manipulate datasets for training and testing machine learning models.

**4. Financial Analysis**
- **Time Series Analysis:** Manage financial data for time series analysis, such as stock prices and economic indicators.

**5. Epidemiology**
- **Tracking Disease Outbreaks:** Analyze the spread of diseases, patient demographics, and treatment outcomes.

**6. Social Science Research**
- **Survey Data Analysis:** Store and analyze survey responses, demographic information, and research study results.

**Summary**
- **Data Frame**: A two-dimensional data structure in R, similar to a table, where data is organized in rows and columns.
- **Column Heterogeneity**: The ability of data frames to store different types of data in each column.
- **Row Homogeneity**: Each row represents a single observation in a data frame.
- **Versatility**: The ability to handle different data types within the same structure.
- **Comprehensive Functionality**: The wide range of functions available for manipulating data frames.
- **Data Cleaning**: The process of detecting and correcting (or removing) corrupt or inaccurate records from a dataset.
- **Subsetting**: Selecting a portion of a data frame based on conditions or indices.
- **Sorting**: Arranging data in a particular order based on column values.
- **Merging**: Combining two data frames based on common columns.

**Glossary**
- **Aggregation**: Summarizing data using functions like mean, sum, or count.
- **Conversion**: Changing the data type of columns or transforming the data frame into another structure.
- **apply/lapply/sapply/tapply/mapply**: Functions in R used to apply other functions to elements of a data frame or list.
- **Tibble**: A modern take on data frames in R, providing cleaner printing and better handling of large data frames.
- **Descriptive Statistics**: Statistical measures that describe the basic features of data.
- **Time Series Analysis**: Techniques used to analyze time-ordered data points.
- **Epidemiology**: The study of the distribution and determinants of health-related states in specified populations.
- **Survey Data Analysis**: The process of analyzing data collected from surveys to draw conclusions about the surveyed population.

## Exercise

**Exercise 1 – Multiple choice questions**
**1.** What is a key characteristic of data frames in R?
**a.** Only numeric data
**b.** Only character data
**c.** Column heterogeneity
**d.** Row heterogeneity

**2.** Which function is used to combine vectors into a data frame?
**a.** c()
**b.** list()
**c.** matrix()
**d.** data.frame()

**Exercise 2 – Fill in the blanks**
1. Data frames in R are similar to tables in a _______ or an Excel spreadsheet.

2. The _______ function is used to apply a function to rows or columns of a data frame.

**Exercise 3 – True or False**
1. Data frames can only contain numeric data.
2. The rbind() function is used to add a new row to a data frame.

**Exercise 4 – Short question answers**
1. What are the key characteristics of a data frame in R?
2. Describe how to access a specific element in a data frame.

**Exercise 5 – Long question answers**
1. Explain in detail how to create and verify a data frame in R..
2. Discuss various methods to modify a data frame in R.

## Answers

**Exercise 1** – 1. c) 2. d)
**Exercise 2** – 1. database 2. apply
**Exercise 3** – 1. False 2. True

**Online Resources**

**Practice Paper**
**Link** : https://forms.gle/eREwamQtRztzm7cX6
**QR Code**

**Project Video**
**Link:** https://www.youtube.com/playlist?list=PLzlh_31VWEFqz3lgly54-ZbzbOcep_Fgv
**QR Code**

**YouTube Video Playlist Link**

**Link**
https://www.youtube.com/playlist?list=PLzlh_31VWEFqz3lgly54-ZbzbOcep_Fgv
**QR Code**

**Test Paper**

**Chapter-10**
**Data Frames**

**Time Duration: 40 Minutes** **Maximum Marks: 25**

**General Instructions:**
1. The question paper consists of 12 questions and is divided into four sections, A, B, C and D.
2. All questions are compulsory.
3. Section A comprises MCQs, Fill in the blanks and True or False carrying one marks each.
4. Section B comprises VSAQs(very short answers questions) carrying two marks each.
5. Section C comprises SAQs(short questions) carrying four marks each.
6. Section D comprises long questions carrying five marks each.

## SECTION-A

**I. Multiple choice questions:** **(1*2=2)**

1. How do you access the 'Age' column in a data frame named students_df?
a. students_df["Age"]
b. students_df$Age
c. students_df(Age)
d. students_df@Age

2. Which function applies a function to each element of a list or data frame and returns a list?
a. apply()
b. lapply()
c. sapply()
d. tapply()

**II. Fill in the blanks:** **(1*2=2)**
1. Tibbles provide a cleaner print method and better support for _______ data frames.
2. The _______ function applies a function to each element of a list or data frame and returns a simplified result.

**III. True or False:** **(1*2=2)**
1. The apply() function returns a data frame as its result.
2. Data frames cannot handle missing values.

## SECTION-B

**IV. Very Short answers type questions-I** **(2*3=6)**
1. What function is used to create a data frame in R?
2. Name one advantage of using data frames.
3. How do you remove a column in a data frame?

## SECTION-C

**V. Short answers type questions-II** **(4*2=8)**
1. Explain how to add a new row to a data frame.
2. What is the difference between lapply() and sapply() functions?

## SECTION-D

**VI. Long answers type questions** **(5*1=5)**
1. Describe the different applications of data frames in various fields.

# Chapter 11: Data frames

**In this chapter you will learn about:**
- Introduction to Graphs
- Creating Graphs
- Histograms and Density Plots
- Dot Plots
- Bar Plots
- Line Charts
- Pie Charts
- Box Plots
- Scatter Plots
- Saving Graphs to a File
- Creating Three-Dimensional Plots Exercises

**Graphs**

Data visualization is a crucial aspect of data analysis, allowing you to communicate insights and patterns in your data effectively. In R, there are several powerful tools and packages available for creating a wide variety of graphs and plots. This introduction will cover the basics of why visualization is important, the primary packages used for creating graphs in R, and the foundational functions and techniques for starting your visualization journey.

**Importance of Data Visualization**

Data visualization serves several key purposes:
- **Understanding Data:** Visuals help in grasping large datasets quickly and identifying patterns, trends, and outliers.
- **Communicating Insights:** Effective visuals convey complex data insights to others in a clear and accessible manner.
- **Decision Making:** Visualizations aid in making data-driven decisions by presenting data in an easily interpretable format.

**Key Concepts in ggplot2**
- **Data**: The dataset being visualized.
- **Aesthetics (aes)**: Mapping data variables to visual properties (e.g., x-axis, y-axis, color).
- **Geometries (geom)**: The type of plot (e.g., points, lines, bars).
- **Layers**: Building the plot layer by layer by adding geometries, scales, and themes.
- **Themes**: Customizing non-data elements (e.g., text, background).

## 11.1 Create Graphs in R

### 11.1.1 Install and Load Necessary Packages:

Before you can create graphs in R, you need to install and load the necessary packages. The most commonly used package for data visualization in R is ggplot2. For base R graphics, no additional package is needed.

```
install.packages("ggplot2")
library(ggplot2)
```

### 11.1.2 Prepare Your Data:

Ensure your data is in the correct format. Data should be in a data frame with appropriate column names. For example, if you are plotting a scatter plot, you should have two columns representing the x and y variables.

```
data <- data.frame(
  x = rnorm(100),
  y = rnorm(100)
)
```

← Sample data

### 11.1.3 Create the Graph:

Depending on the type of graph you want to create, use the appropriate function. For base R graphics, functions like plot(), hist(), and barplot() are used. For ggplot2, you use the ggplot() function along with specific geom_* functions.

```
plot(data$x, data$y, main="Base R Scatter
Plot", xlab="X Axis", ylab="Y Axis")        <-- Base R example - scatter plot

 ggplot(data, aes(x = x, y = y)) +          <-- ggplot2 example - scatter plot
 geom_point() +
 ggtitle("ggplot2 Scatter Plot") +
 xlab("X Axis") +
 ylab("Y Axis")
```

**Output:**

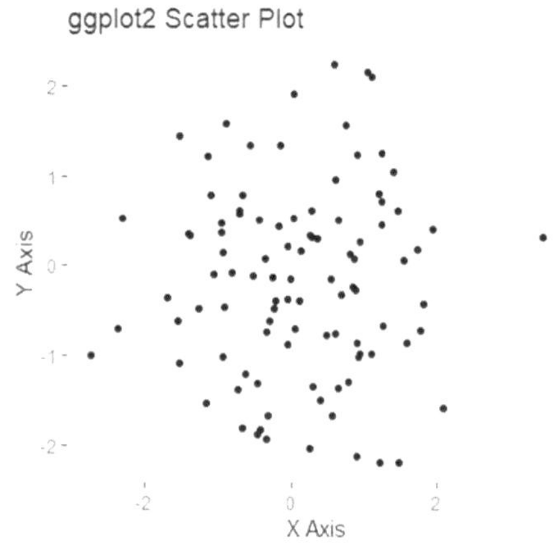


### 11.1.4 Customize the Graph:

Customize the appearance of your graph by adding titles, labels, colors, and themes. Both base R and ggplot2 offer extensive customization options.

```
plot(data$x, data$y, main="Customized Base R Scatter Plot", xlab="X Axis", ylab="Y Axis",
col="blue", pch=16)

ggplot(data, aes(x = x, y = y)) +
  geom_point(color = "blue", size = 3) +
  ggtitle("Customized ggplot2 Scatter Plot") +
  xlab("X Axis") +
  ylab("Y Axis") +
  theme_minimal()
```

**Output:**

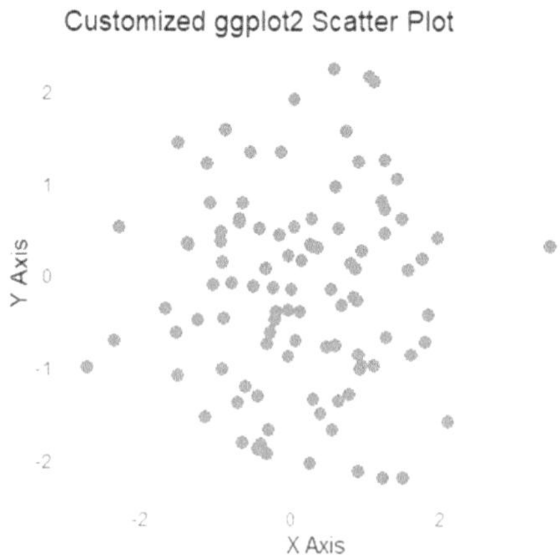


### 11.1.5 Save the Graph:

Save your graph to a file for use in reports or presentations. Both base R and ggplot2 provide functions to save plots.

```
png("base_r_scatter_plot.png")
plot(data$x, data$y, main="Base R Scatter Plot", xlab="X Axis", ylab="Y Axis")
dev.off()
```

**Output:**

```
RStudioGD
        2
```

```
ggsave("ggplot2_scatter_plot.png")
```

**Output:**

```
Saving 3.99 x 3.74 in image
```

**11.2 Introduction to ggplot2**

ggplot2 is a powerful and flexible R package for creating elegant data visualizations. It implements the "Grammar of Graphics" by Leland Wilkinson, which provides a systematic way to describe and build graphs.

**11.2.1 Basic Structure of ggplot2:**

The core function of ggplot2 is ggplot(), which initializes the graph. You then add layers to this plot using + and specific geom_* functions to represent different types of plots.

```
library(ggplot2)
data <- data.frame(
  x = rnorm(100),
  y = rnorm(100)
)
ggplot(data, aes(x = x, y = y)) +
  geom_point()
```

**Output:**

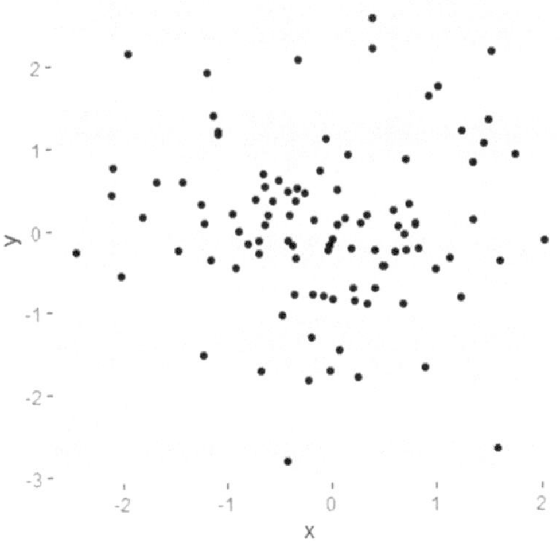


**11.2.2 Aesthetic Mappings (aes):**

The aes() function is used to map variables in your data to visual properties (aesthetics) such as x and y positions, colors, and sizes.

```
ggplot(data, aes(x = x, y = y, color = x)) +
  geom_point()
```

**Output:**

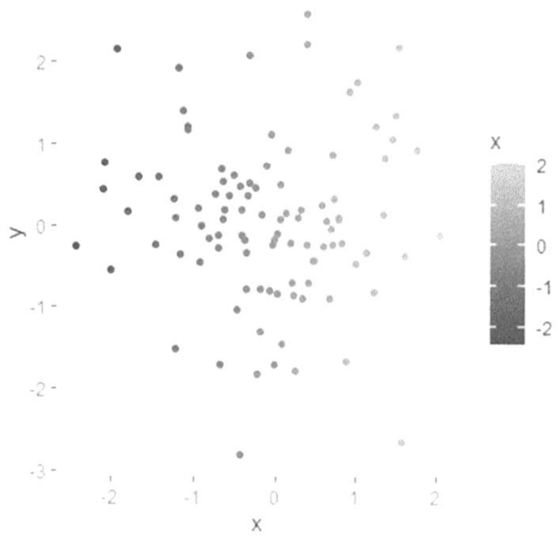


### 11.2.3 Geometric Objects (geom_*):

Geometric objects (geom_*) define the type of plot you are creating. Common geom_* functions include geom_point() for scatter plots, geom_line() for line charts, geom_bar() for bar plots, and geom_histogram() for histograms.

```
ggplot(data, aes(x = x, y = y)) +
geom_point() +
  geom_smooth(method = "lm", se = FALSE)
```

**Output:** geom_smooth()` using formula = 'y ~ x'

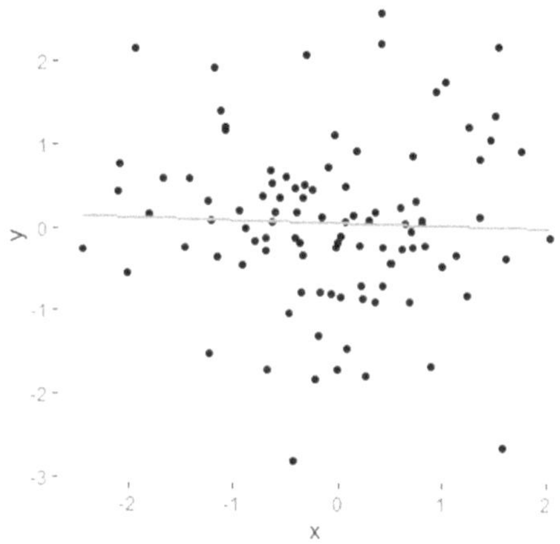


### 11.2.4 Faceting:

Faceting allows you to split your data into subsets and display these subsets in different panels within the same plot. This is useful for comparing groups.

```
data$group <- sample(letters[1:3], 100, replace = TRUE)
ggplot(data, aes(x = x, y = y)) +
  geom_point() +
  facet_wrap(~ factor_variable)
```

**Output:**

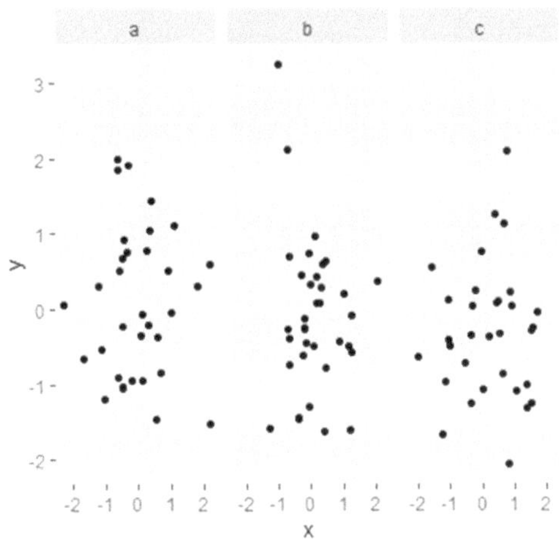


### 11.2.5 Themes and Customization:

ggplot2 provides various themes to enhance the appearance of your plots. You can customize nearly every aspect of your plot using theme functions.

```
ggplot(data, aes(x = x, y = y)) +
  geom_point() +
  ggtitle("Customized ggplot2 Plot") +
  xlab("X Axis") +
  ylab("Y Axis") +
  theme_minimal() +
  theme(plot.title = element_text(hjust = 0.5))
```

**Output:**

### 11.2.6 Saving Plots:

Use ggsave() to save your ggplot2 plots to a file. This function allows you to specify the filename, format, and dimensions of the saved plot.

```
ggplot(data, aes(x = x, y = y)) +
  geom_point() +
  ggtitle("ggplot2 Plot")
ggsave("ggplot2_plot.png", width = 6, height = 4)
```

**Output:**

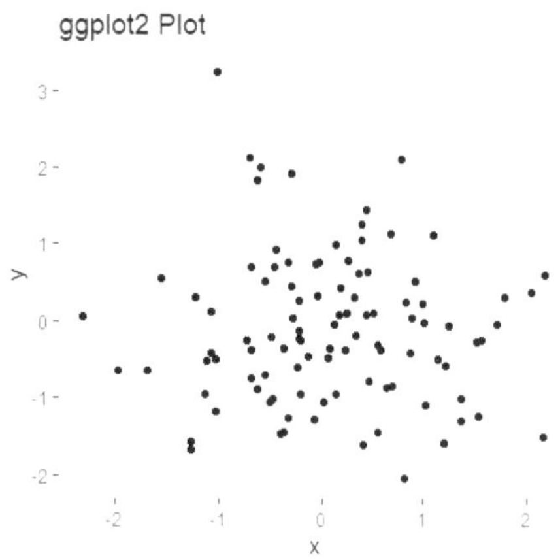


### 11.3. Histograms

A histogram is a graphical representation of the distribution of a dataset. It divides the data into bins and shows the frequency or count of data points in each bin. Histograms are useful for understanding the shape, central tendency, and variability of the data.

**11.3.1 Creating Histograms Using hist():** The hist() function in base R is used to create histograms. Here is a step-by-step guide:

```
data <- rnorm(1000, mean = 50, sd = 10)

hist(data, main="Histogram of Data", xlab="Value", ylab="Frequency")
```

← Sample data

← Creating a basic histogram

**Output:**

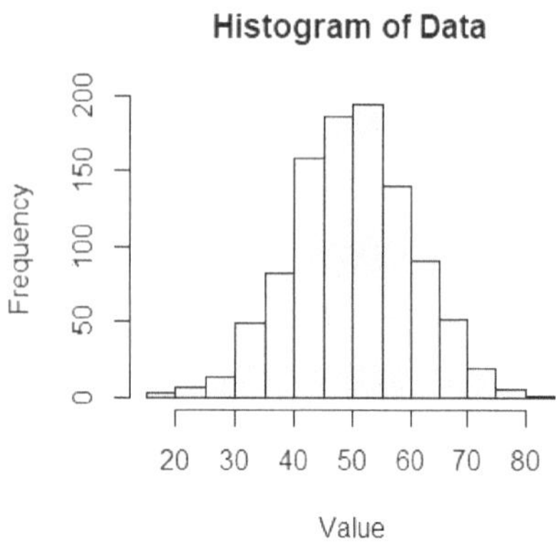


**11.3.2 Customizing Bins:**

```
hist(data, breaks=20, main="Histogram with Custom Bins", xlab="Value", ylab="Frequency")
```

**Output:**

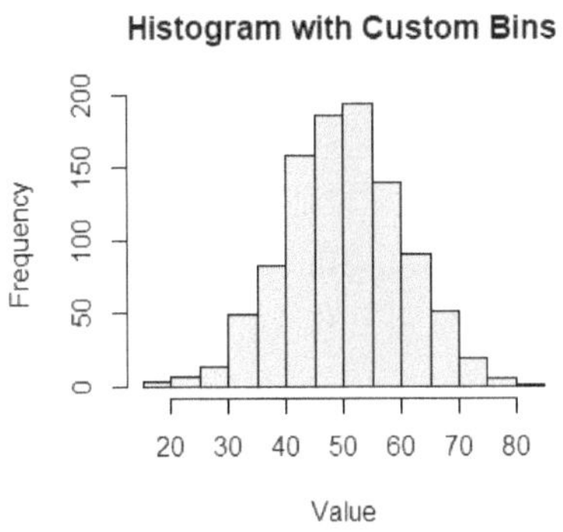


### 11.3.4 Adding Colors and Labels:

```
hist(data, breaks=20, col="blue", main="Colored Histogram", xlab="Value", ylab="Frequency")
```

**Output:**

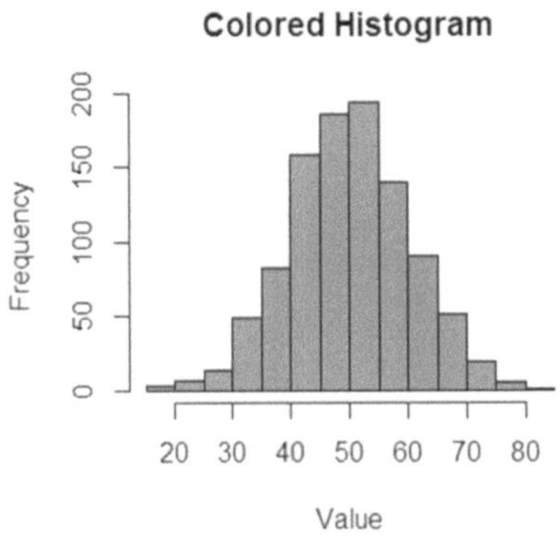


### 11.3.5 Overlaying a Density Plot:

```
hist(data, breaks=20, col="gray", main="Histogram with Density Plot", xlab="Value", ylab="Density",
freq=FALSE)
lines(density(data), col="red", lwd=2)
```

**Output:**

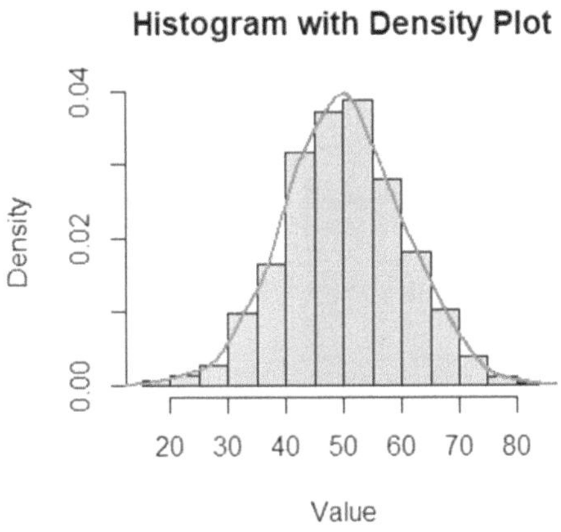

**11.3.5 When to Use Histogram:**
- Use histograms when you need a simple and clear representation of the frequency distribution.
- They are particularly useful when dealing with discrete data or when you want to show the number of observations within specific intervals.

### 11.4 Density Plots

A density plot is a smoothed version of a histogram, which estimates the probability density function of the data. Density plots are useful for visualizing the distribution of a dataset.

**Creating Density Plots Using density():** The density() function in base R is used to create density plots. Here is a step-by-step guide:

#### 11.4.1 Basic Density Plot:

```
data <- rnorm(1000, mean = 50, sd = 10)
hist(data, main="Histogram of Data", xlab="Value", ylab="Frequency")
```

Sample data

Creating a basic density plot

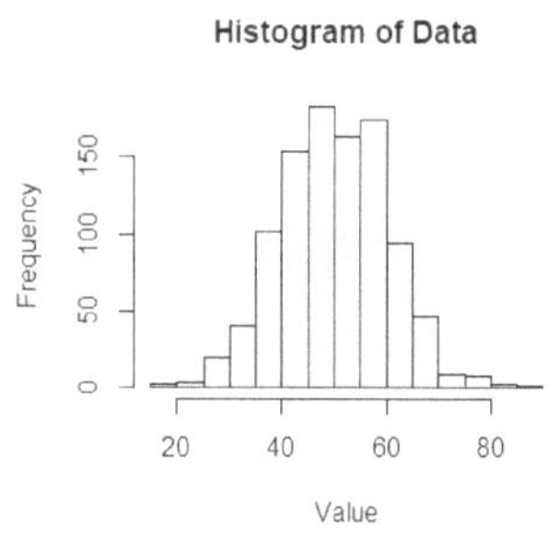


#### 11.4.2 Adding Colors and Lines:

```
density_data <- density(data)
plot(density_data, main="Density Plot with Customizations",
 xlab="Value", ylab="Density", col="blue", lwd=2)
```

**Output:**

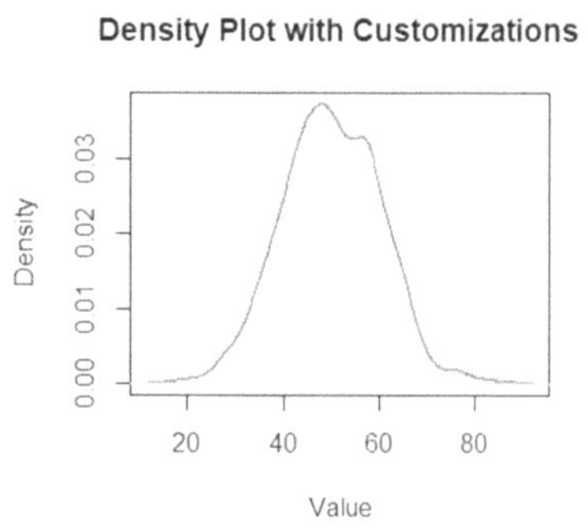


#### 11.4.3 Overlaying on a Histogram:

```
hist(data, breaks=20, col="gray", main="Histogram with Density Plot",
 xlab="Value", ylab="Density", freq=FALSE)
lines(density(data), col="red", lwd=2)
```

**Output:**

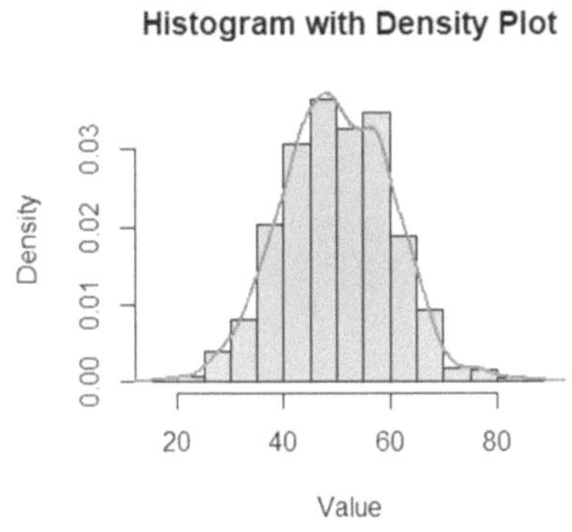


### 11.4.4 When to use Density Plot:

- Use density plots when you want a smooth and continuous representation of the data's distribution.
- They are ideal for visualizing continuous data and comparing multiple distributions.
- Density plots are useful when you are interested in understanding the overall shape and spread of the data rather than exact frequencies.

## 11.5 Dot Plot

Dot plots are a simple way to visualize individual data points. They are particularly useful for small to moderate-sized datasets and can help identify the distribution and spread of the data. In R, you can create dot plots using both base R functions and the ggplot2 package.

### 11.5.1 Basic Dot Plot with dotchart():

```
data <- c(5, 7, 8, 5, 6, 9, 5, 7, 8, 9)                                          ← Sample data
dotchart(data, main = "Basic Dot Plot", xlab = "Value", ylab = "Index")          ← Create a basic dot plot
```

**Output:**

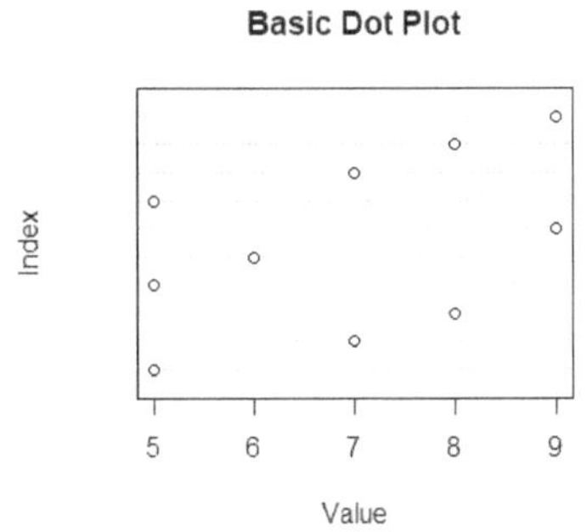


### 11.5.2 Dot Plot with Categories:

```
categories <- factor(c("A", "B", "A", "B", "C", "A", "C", "B", "C", "A"))
values <- c(5, 7, 8, 5, 6, 9, 5, 7, 8, 9)
dotchart(values, labels = categories, main = "Dot Plot with Categories", xlab = "Value", ylab = "Category")
```

**Output:**

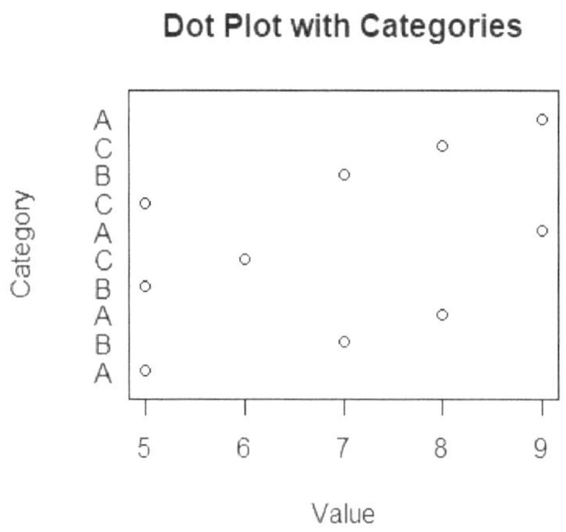


### 11.5.3 Customized Dot Plot:

```
dotchart(values, labels = categories, main = "Customized Dot Plot",
xlab = "Value", ylab = "Category", col = "blue", pch = 19)
```

**Output:**

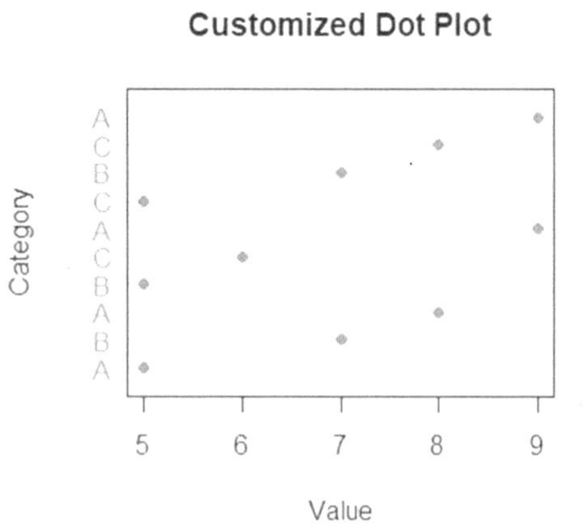


## 11.6 Bar Plots

Bar plots are a common way to visualize categorical data. They display rectangular bars with lengths proportional to the values they represent. In R, bar plots can be created using both the base R functions and the ggplot2 package.

**Creating Bar Plots using Base R**

**11.6.1 Basic Bar Plot:** The simplest way to create a bar plot in R is using the barplot() function.

```
counts <- c(10, 20, 15, 30)
categories <- c("A", "B", "C", "D")

barplot(counts, names.arg = categories, col = "blue", main = "Basic Bar Plot", xlab = "Categories", ylab =
"Counts")
```

**Output:**

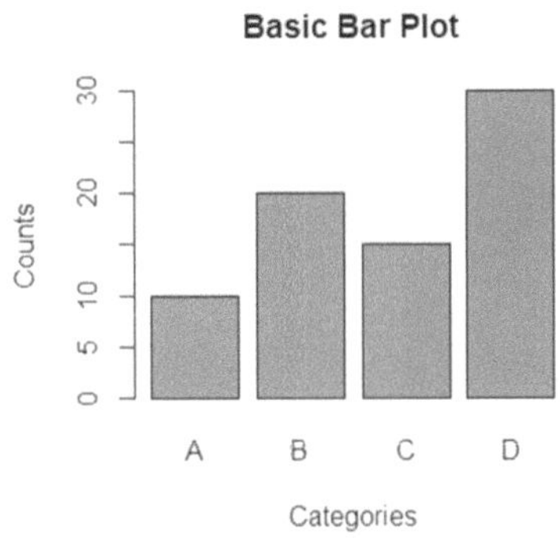


**11.6.1 Grouped Bar Plot:** Grouped bar plots are useful when you want to compare different groups side by side.

```
counts <- matrix(c(10, 15, 20, 25, 30, 35, 40, 45), nrow = 2, byrow = TRUE)
categories <- c("A", "B", "C", "D")

barplot(counts, beside = TRUE, names.arg = categories, col = c("blue", "red"), main = "Grouped Bar Plot",
xlab = "Categories", ylab = "Counts", legend = rownames(counts))
```

**Output:**

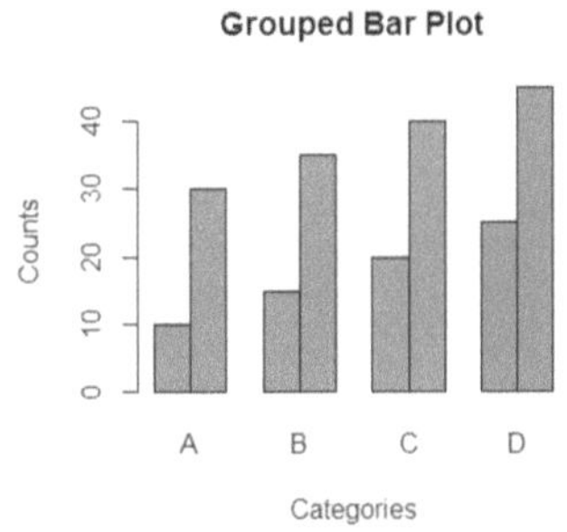


**11.6.2 Stacked Bar Plot:** Stacked bar plots are useful to show the total value across different categories along with the individual segment contributions.

```
counts <- matrix(c(10, 15, 20, 25, 30, 35, 40, 45), nrow = 2, byrow = TRUE)
categories <- c("A", "B", "C", "D")

barplot(counts, beside = FALSE, names.arg = categories, col = c("blue", "red"), main = "Stacked Bar Plot",
xlab = "Categories", ylab = "Counts", legend = rownames(counts))
```

**Output:**

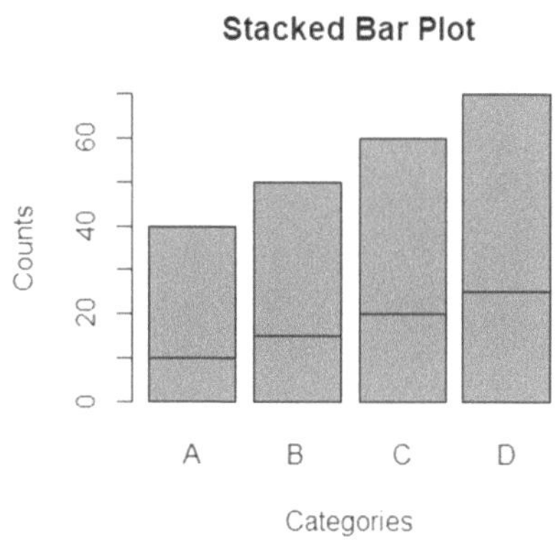


**11.6.3 Customizing Bar Plots:** You can customize bar plots by adding titles, axis labels, colors, and legends.

```
counts <- c(10, 20, 15, 30)
categories <- c("A", "B", "C", "D")

barplot(counts, names.arg = categories, col = "green", main = "Customized Bar Plot", xlab = "Categories",
ylab = "Counts", border = "red", density = 20)
```

**Output:**

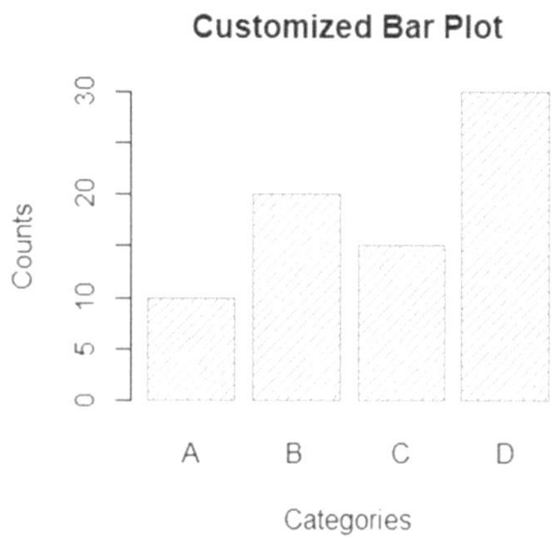


### 11.7 Line Charts

Line charts are a type of graph used to display information as a series of data points connected by straight line segments. They are particularly useful for visualizing trends over time. In R, line charts can be created using both the base R plotting functions and the ggplot2 package. Below is a detailed guide on creating line charts in R.

**Using Base R**

#### 11.7.1 Basic Line Chart

```
x <- c(1, 2, 3, 4, 5)
y <- c(2, 3, 5, 7, 11)

plot(x, y, type = "l", col = "blue", xlab = "X-axis", ylab = "Y-axis", main = "Basic Line Chart")
```

**Output:**

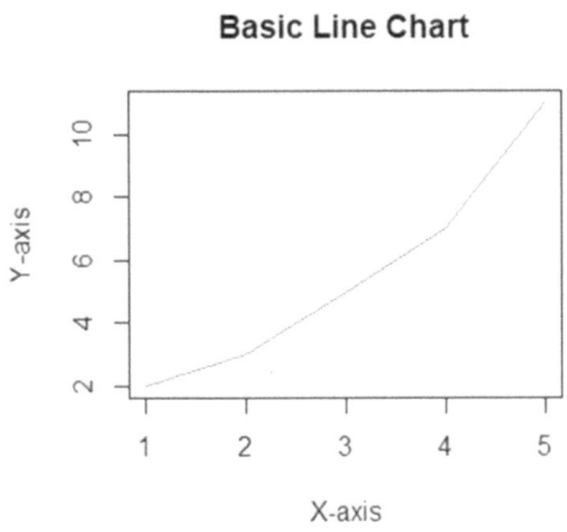


1. Adding Points and Customizing Lines

```
plot(x, y, type = "b", col = "blue", xlab = "X-axis", ylab = "Y-axis", main
= "Line Chart with Points")

plot(x, y, type = "l", col = "red", lty = 2, lwd = 2, xlab = "X-axis", ylab =
"Y-axis", main = "Customized Line Chart")
```

**Output:**

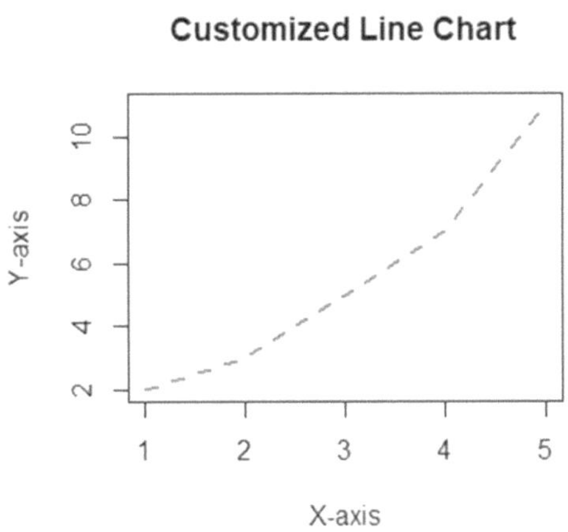


**11.7.2 Adding Multiple Lines**

```
y2 <- c(1, 4, 6, 8, 10)

plot(x, y, type = "l", col = "blue", xlab = "X-axis", ylab = "Y-axis", main = "Multiple Lines Chart")
lines(x, y2, type = "l", col = "red", lty = 2)
legend("topleft", legend = c("Line 1", "Line 2"), col = c("blue", "red"), lty = 1:2)
```

**Output:**

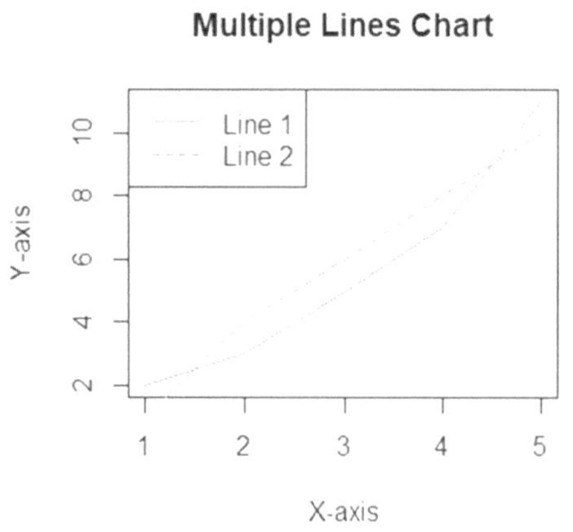


### 11.8 Pie Charts
Pie charts are a circular statistical graphic divided into slices to illustrate numerical proportions. In R, you can create pie charts using both base R functions and packages like ggplot2. This detailed guide will cover creating and customizing pie charts in R.

**11.8.1 Creating Pie Charts:** The base R function pie() is used to create pie charts.

```
slices <- c(10, 20, 30, 40)
labels <- c("Category A", "Category B", "Category C", "Category D")

pie(slices, labels = labels, main = "Pie Chart Example")
```

**Output:**

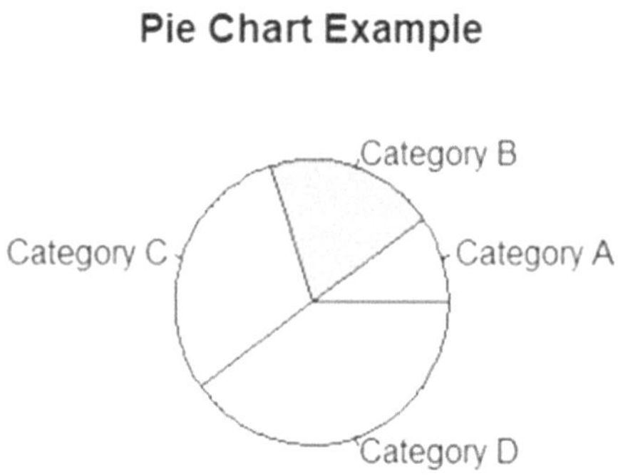


**11.8.2 Customizations:**
- **Colors:** Use the col parameter to specify colors.
- **Exploding Slices:** Use the explode parameter to pull slices out from the center.
- **Adding Percentages:** Calculate percentages and add them to the labels.

```
colors <- c("red", "blue", "green", "yellow")

percentages <- round(slices / sum(slices) * 100)

# Add percentages to labels
labels_with_percentages <- paste(labels, percentages, "%")

pie(slices, labels = labels_with_percentages, col = colors, main = "Customized Pie Chart")
```

**Output:**

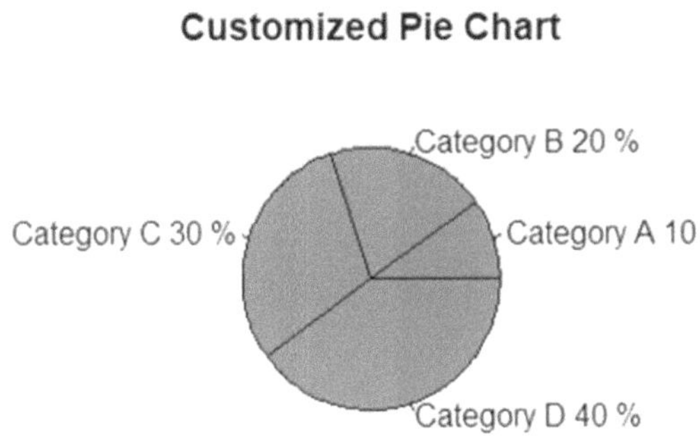


**11.9 Box Plots**

Box plots, also known as box-and-whisker plots, are a standard way of displaying the distribution of data based on a five-number summary: minimum, first quartile (Q1), median, third quartile (Q3), and maximum. They are particularly useful for identifying outliers and understanding the spread and skewness of the data.

**Creating Box Plots:** In base R, the boxplot() function is used to create box plots. Here's how you can create and customize box plots in base R.

**11.9.1 Basic Box Plot**

```
data <- c(10, 15, 14, 18, 20, 22, 24, 25, 30, 32, 35, 40, 42, 45, 48, 50, 55, 60)

boxplot(data, main="Basic Box Plot", ylab="Values")
```

**Output:**

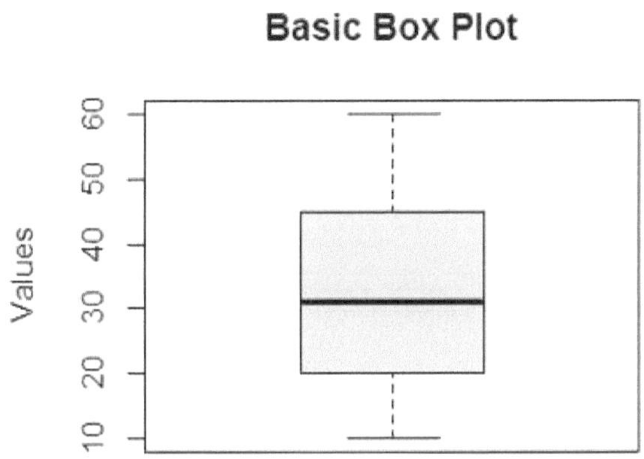


**11.9.2 Box Plot for Multiple Groups**

```
group1 <- c(10, 15, 14, 18, 20)
group2 <- c(22, 24, 25, 30, 32)
group3 <- c(35, 40, 42, 45, 48)
data <- data.frame(Group=c(rep("Group1", 5), rep("Group2", 5), rep("Group3", 5)), Values=c(group1,
group2, group3))

boxplot(Values ~ Group, data=data, main="Box Plot for Multiple Groups", ylab="Values")
```

**Output:**

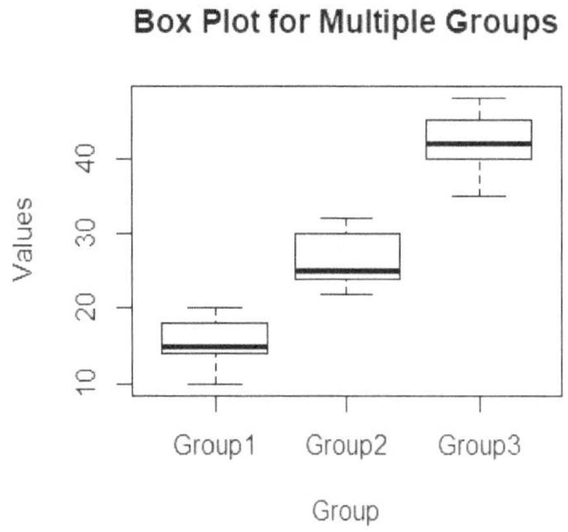


**11.9.3 Customizing Box Plots:** You can customize box plots with various parameters like colors, notch, outline, and more.

```
boxplot(Values ~ Group, data=data,
    main="Customized Box Plot",
    ylab="Values",
    col=c("red", "green", "blue"),
    notch=FALSE,
    outline=FALSE)
```

**Output:**

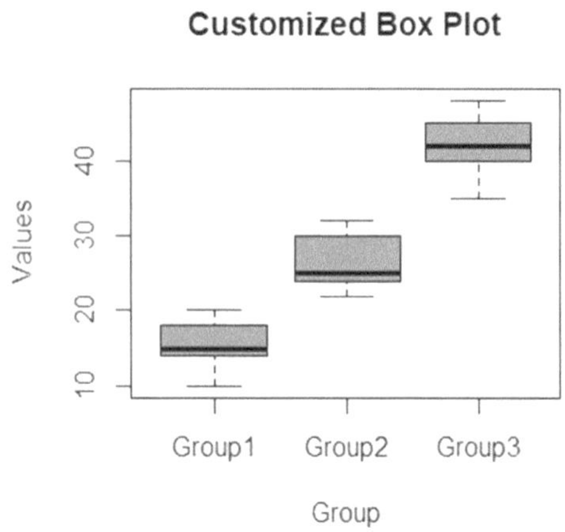


**11.10 Scatter Plot**

Scatter plots are used to display the relationship between two continuous variables. They are an essential tool in data analysis and visualization, providing insights into correlations, trends, and potential outliers. In R, scatter plots can be created using both base R functions and the ggplot2 package.

**Creating Scatter Plots with Base R**

**11.10.1 Basic Scatter Plot**

```
x <- rnorm(100)
y <- rnorm(100)

plot(x, y, main="Basic Scatter Plot", xlab="X-axis", ylab="Y-axis", pch=19, col="blue")
```

**Output:**

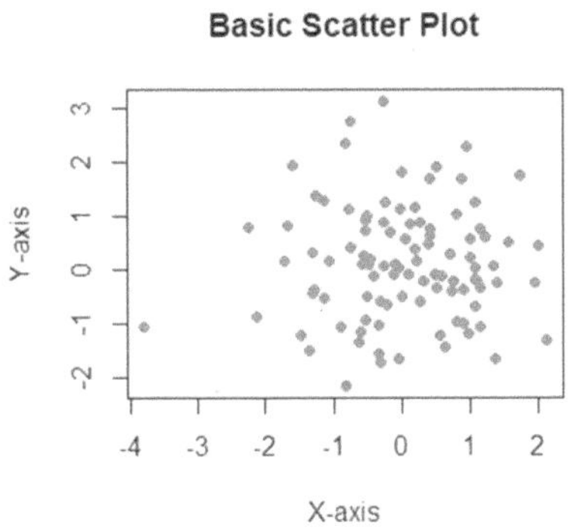


### 11.10.2 Adding Titles and Labels

```
plot(x, y, main="Scatter Plot with Labels", xlab="X-axis Label", ylab="Y-axis Label", pch=19, col="blue"
```

**Output:**

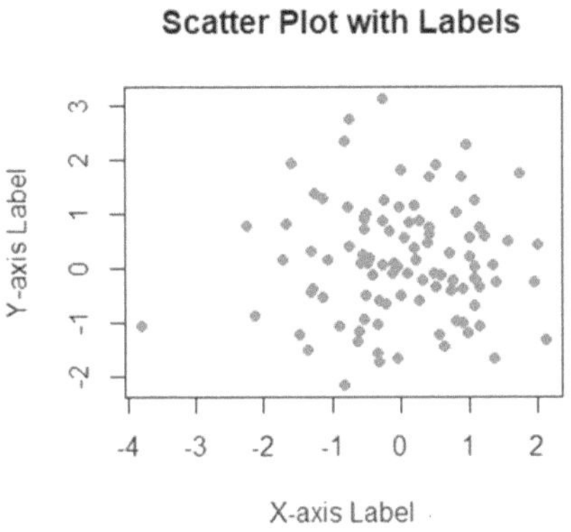


### 11.10.3 Customizing Points

```
plot(x, y, main="Scatter Plot with Custom Points", xlab="X-axis", ylab="Y-axis", pch=16, col="red")
points(rnorm(50), rnorm(50), pch=17, col="green")
points(rnorm(30), rnorm(30), pch=18, col="blue")
```

**Output:**

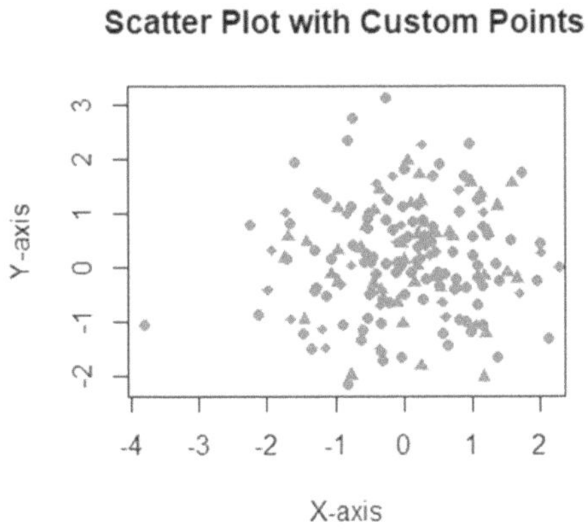


### 11.10.4 Adding a Regression Line

```
plot(x, y, main="Scatter Plot with Custom Points", xlab="X-axis", ylab="Y-axis", pch=16, col="red")
points(rnorm(50), rnorm(50), pch=17, col="green")
points(rnorm(30), rnorm(30), pch=18, col="blue")
```

**Output:**

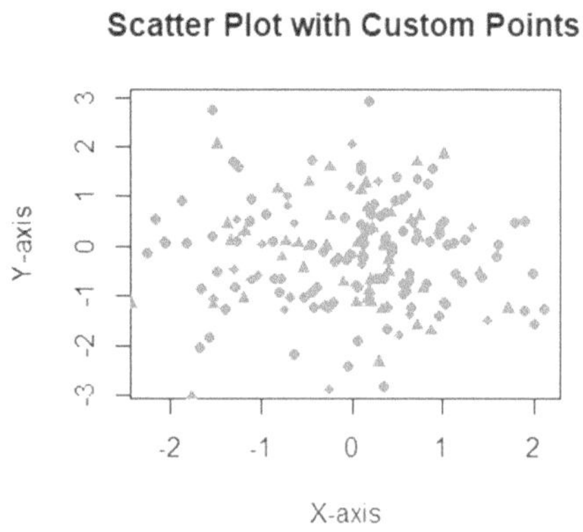


### 11.10.5 Adding Text Labels

```
plot(x, y, main="Scatter Plot with Text Labels", xlab="X-axis", ylab="Y-axis", pch=19, col="blue")
text(x, y, labels=1:100, pos=4, cex=0.6, col="darkgreen")
```

**Output:**

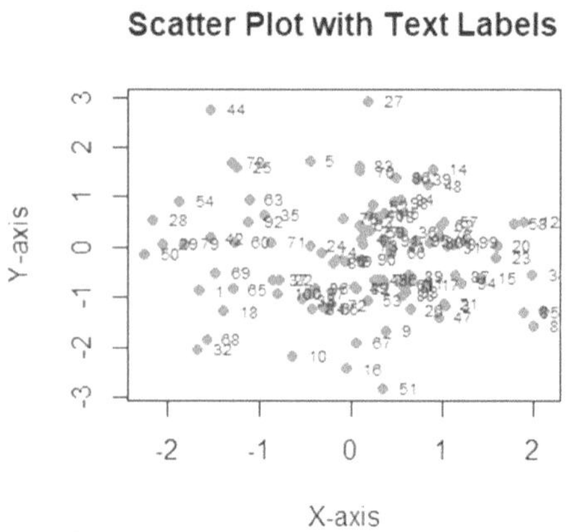


## 11.11 Saving Graphs to a File

Saving graphs to a file is an important step when you want to preserve your visualizations for reports, presentations, or further analysis. R provides several functions and methods to save graphs in different formats, such as PNG, PDF, JPEG, TIFF, and more. Below is a detailed guide on how to save graphs in R using various methods.

**11.11.1 Using ggsave() with ggplot2:** ggsave() is the most common and convenient function for saving graphs created with ggplot2. It automatically saves the last plot that you created or a specified plot object.

- Basic Syntax:

```
ggsave(filename, plot = last_plot(), device = NULL, path = NULL, scale = 1, width = NA, height = NA, units = c("in", "cm", "mm"), dpi = 300, limitsize = TRUE)
```

- Example:
library(ggplot2)
p <- ggplot(mtcars, aes(x = wt, y = mpg)) + geom_point()

ggsave("scatter_plot.png", plot = p)

**Output:**
Saving 3.99 x 3.74 in image

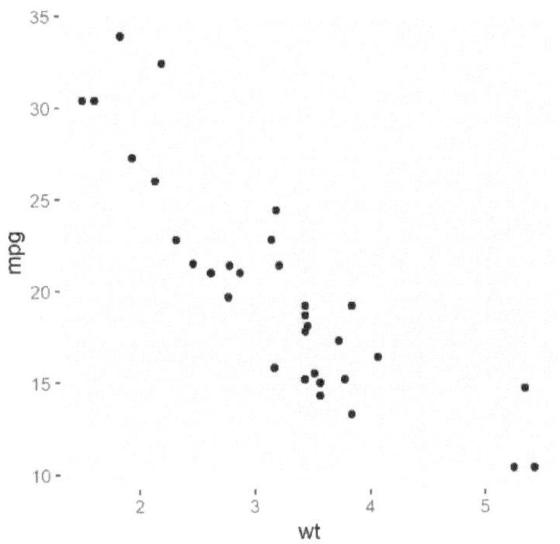


- Parameters:

- **filename:** The name of the output file, including the extension (e.g., "plot.png").
- **plot:** The plot object you want to save. By default, it saves the last plot.
- **device:** The format to save the plot in, e.g., "png", "pdf", "jpeg".
- **path:** The directory path to save the file. If not specified, it saves in the current working directory.
- **width, height:** The width and height of the plot in the specified units.
- **units:** The units for width and height (inches, cm, or mm).
- **dpi:** The resolution of the plot (dots per inch). Common settings are 300 for high quality.

- Customizing Plot Size and Format:

ggsave("scatter_plot.pdf", plot = p, width = 8, height = 6, units = "in")

**Output:**

**11.11.2 Using png(), jpeg(), tiff(), pdf() Functions:** These functions are part of the base R graphics package and are used to open a graphical device that saves all plots generated between the function call and dev.off() to a file.

- Saving as PNG:

```
# Open a PNG device
png("plot.png", width = 800, height = 600)

# Create a plot
```

```
plot(mtcars$wt, mtcars$mpg, main = "Scatter Plot", xlab = "Weight", ylab = "MPG")

# Close the device
dev.off()
```

**Output: plot.png**

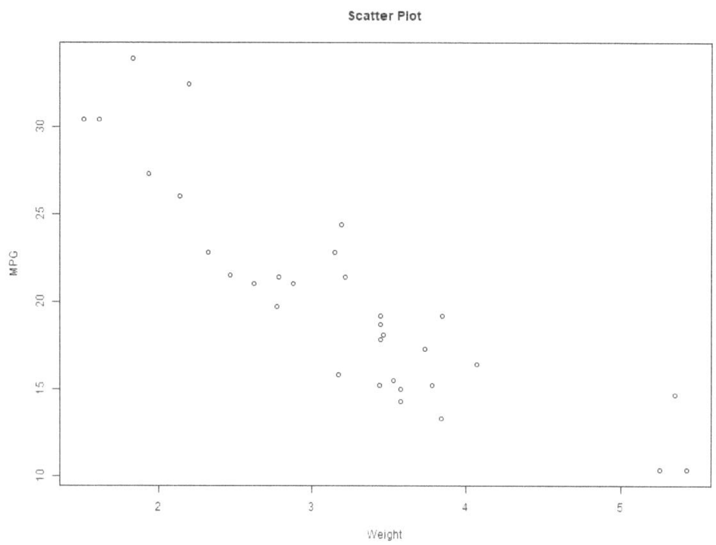


- Saving as PDF:

```
# Open a PDF device
pdf("plot.pdf", width = 8, height = 6)

# Create a plot
plot(mtcars$wt, mtcars$mpg, main = "Scatter Plot", xlab = "Weight", ylab = "MPG")

# Close the device
dev.off()
```

**Output:**

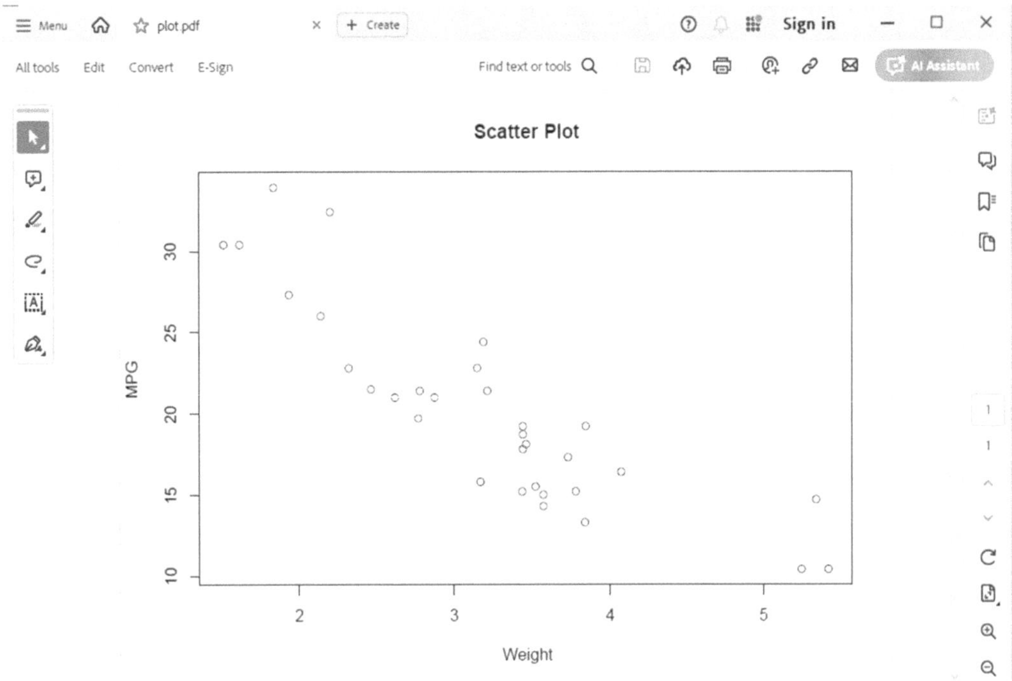


- Saving as JPEG:

```
# Open a JPEG device
jpeg("plot.jpg", width = 800, height = 600, quality = 100)

# Create a plot
plot(mtcars$wt, mtcars$mpg, main = "Scatter Plot", xlab = "Weight", ylab = "MPG")

# Close the device
dev.off()
```

**Output:**

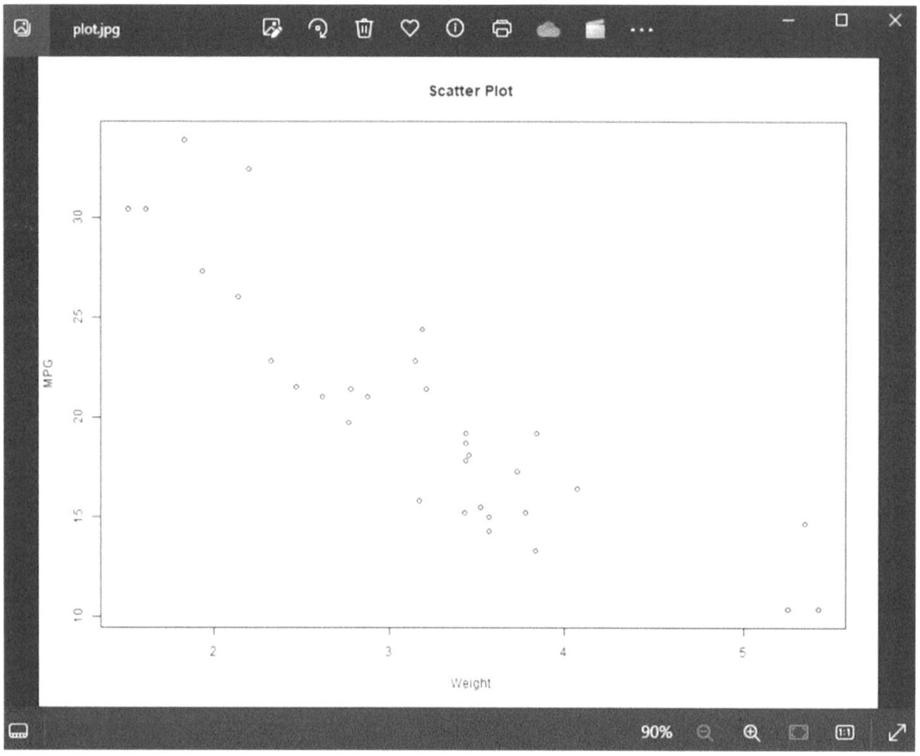


- Saving as TIFF:

```
# Open a TIFF device
tiff("plot.tiff", width = 800, height = 600, res = 300)

# Create a plot
plot(mtcars$wt, mtcars$mpg, main = "Scatter Plot", xlab = "Weight", ylab = "MPG")

# Close the device
dev.off()
```

**Output:**

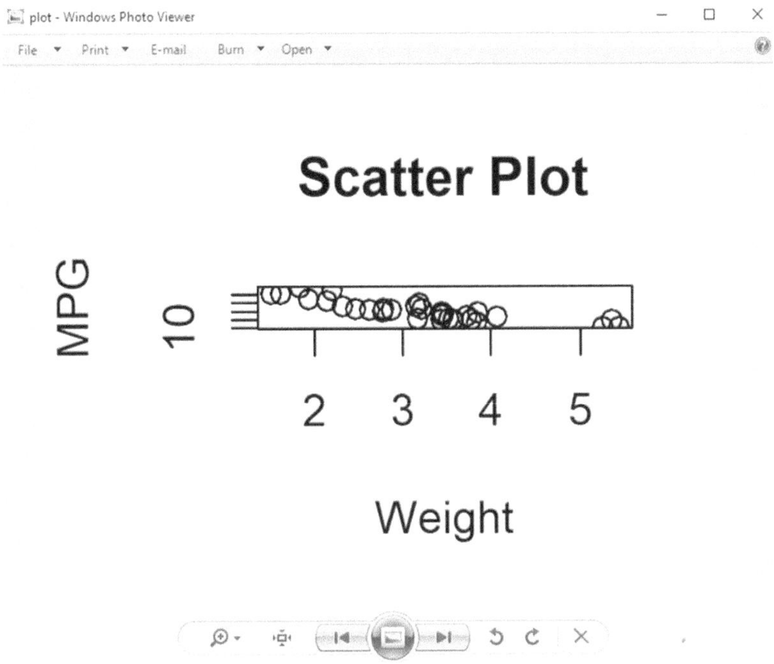


- Parameters:

- filename: The name of the file to save the plot.
- width, height: The dimensions of the plot.
- res: Resolution of the plot for bitmap formats like TIFF.
- quality: For JPEG files, this specifies the quality (0 to 100).

**11.11.3 Using dev.copy() and dev.print():** dev.copy() is used to copy the current plot to a file, and dev.print() is used to send a copy of the plot to a file directly from the screen device.
- Using dev.copy():

```
# Open a TIFF device
tiff("plot.tiff", width = 800, height = 600, res = 300)

# Create a plot
plot(mtcars$wt, mtcars$mpg, main = "Scatter Plot", xlab = "Weight", ylab = "MPG")

# Close the device
dev.off()
```

**Output:**

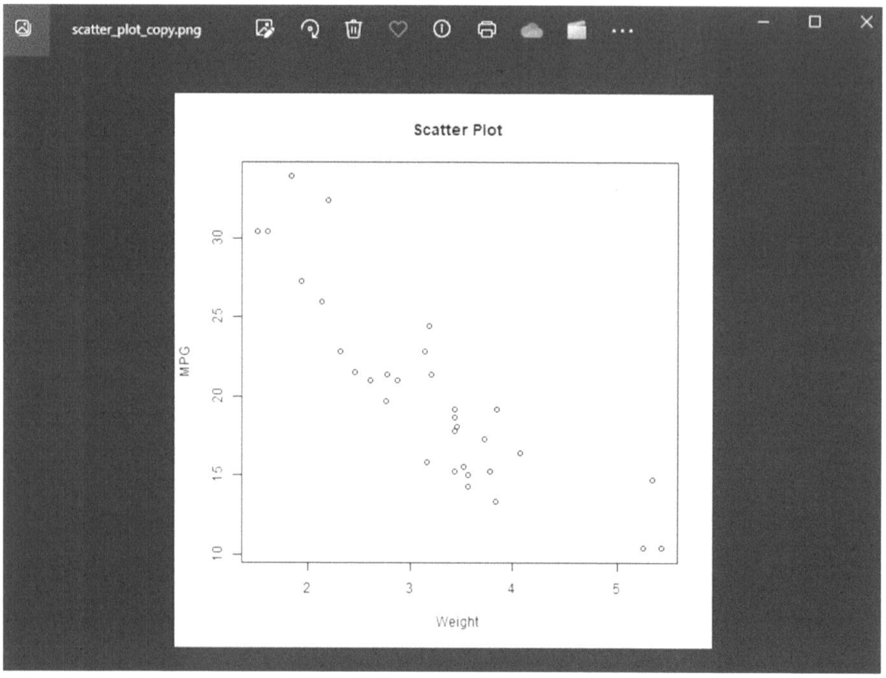


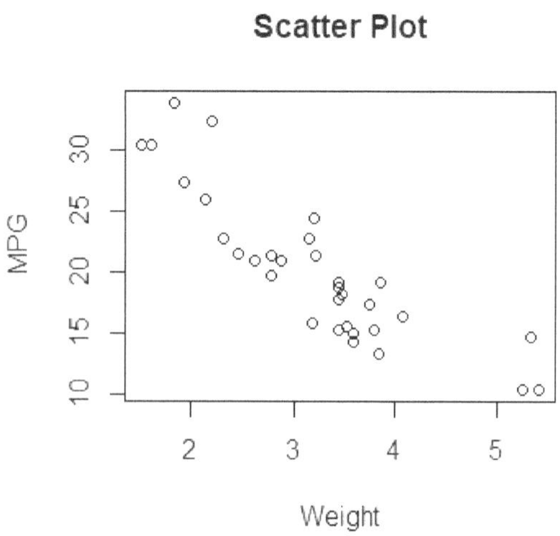


- Using dev.print():

```
# Create a plot
plot(mtcars$wt, mtcars$mpg, main = "Scatter Plot", xlab = "Weight", ylab = "MPG")

# Print the plot to a PDF file
dev.print(pdf, file = "scatter_plot_print.pdf")
dev.off()  # Close the PDF device
```

**Output:**

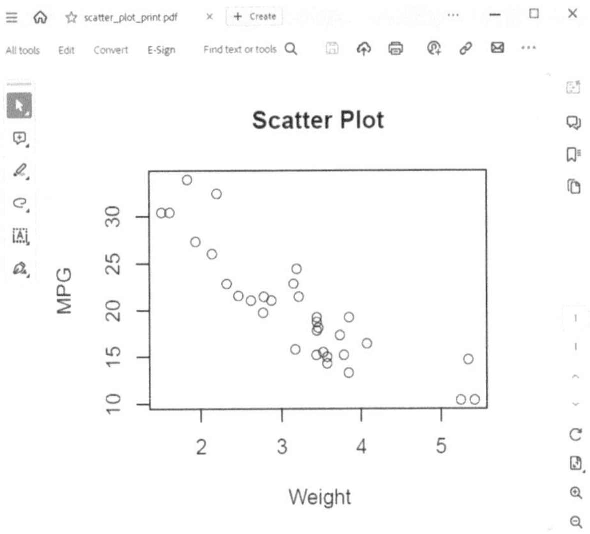


### 11.11.4 Best Practices for Saving Graphs

- **Resolution and Size:** For publication-quality images, set a higher dpi (300 or above) and specify the dimensions using width and height parameters.
- **File Formats:** Use PNG or TIFF for images, PDF for vector graphics and documents, and JPEG for images where file size is a concern, though it might compromise quality.
- **File Naming:** Use descriptive and consistent file names to keep track of your saved plots.

## 11.12 Creating three dimensional plot

Three-dimensional (3D) plots are useful for visualizing data that has more than two variables. In R, there are several packages that enable the creation of 3D plots, including plot3D, rgl, and lattice. Below is a detailed guide on how to create 3D plots in R using Plot 3D packages.

**11.12.1 Using the plot3D Package:** The plot3D package provides a variety of functions for 3D plotting, including scatter plots, surface plots, and contour plots.

- Installation and Loading:

```
install.packages("plot3D")

library(plot3D)
```

- **3D Scatter Plot:** A 3D scatter plot visualizes the relationship between three continuous variables.

```
x <- rnorm(100)
y <- rnorm(100)
z <- rnorm(100)

# 3D scatter plot
scatter3D(x, y, z, colvar = z, col = rainbow(100), pch = 16, cex = 2, xlab = "X Axis", ylab = "Y Axis", zlab
= "Z Axis")
```

**Output:**

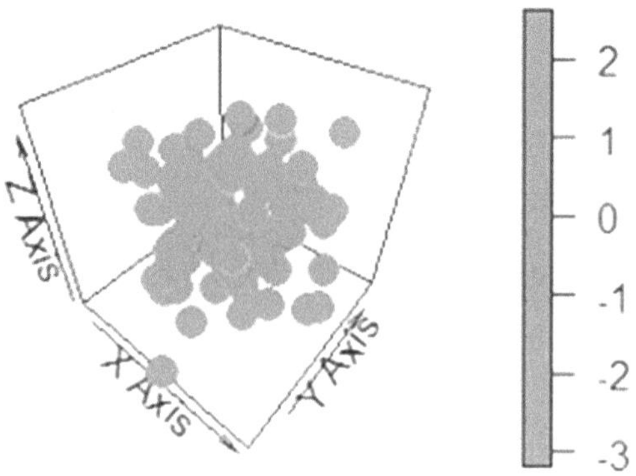


- **3D Surface Plot:** A 3D surface plot displays a three-dimensional surface defined by a function or data.

```
x <- seq(-10, 10, length.out = 50)
y <- seq(-10, 10, length.out = 50)
z <- outer(x, y, function(x, y) cos(sqrt(x^2 + y^2)))

# 3D surface plot
persp3D(x, y, z, theta = 30, phi = 30, expand = 0.5, col = "lightblue")
```

**Output:**

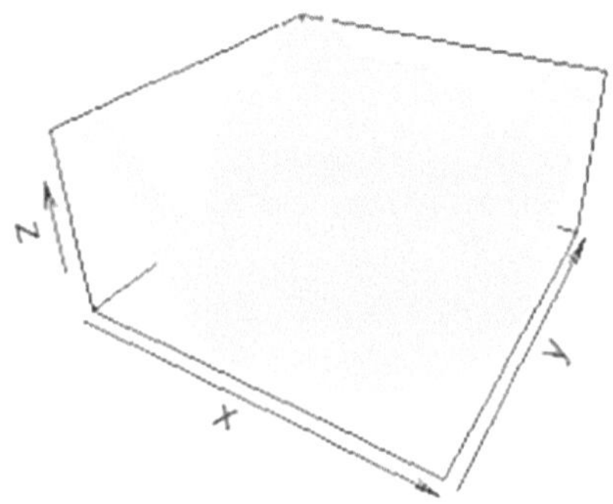


**11.12.2 Best Practices for 3D Plotting**

- **Choose the Right Plot:** Not all data is suitable for 3D visualization. Use 3D plots when the third dimension adds significant value to the interpretation of the data.
- **Label Axes Clearly:** Always label your axes and provide a legend if necessary, to help interpret the plot correctly.
- **Consider Interactivity:** Use interactive plots (e.g., with the rgl package) when the ability to rotate and zoom the plot enhances understanding.
- **Avoid Overcrowding:** Too many data points or lines in a 3D plot can make it difficult to read. Simplify the plot as much as possible.

**11.12.3 Saving and Sharing 3D Plots**

- **Interactive HTML Widgets:** Use the rgl package to save plots as interactive HTML widgets, which can be shared easily.
- **Static Images:** Save your plots as high-quality PNG or PDF files using the appropriate functions (rgl.snapshot(), png()).

**Summary**

- **Data Visualization**: The use of graphical representations to interpret and communicate data insights.
- **ggplot2**: An R package for creating advanced, customizable graphs based on the "Grammar of Graphics."
- **Aesthetics (aes)**: In `ggplot2`, the mapping of data variables to visual attributes like position and color.

- **Geometries (geom)**: Visual elements in `ggplot2`, such as bars, lines, or points that represent data.
- **Layers**: Components in `ggplot2` that stack to build complex visualizations, including data layers and themes.
- **Themes**: Customization options in `ggplot2` that modify non-data elements like text and backgrounds.
- **Histograms**: Plots that show the frequency distribution of data divided into bins.
- **Density Plot**: A smoothed curve representing the probability density of data, similar to a histogram.
- **Dot Plot**: A plot that visualizes individual data points, ideal for small datasets.
- **Bar Plot**: A chart that uses bars to represent categorical data, with bar length proportional to value.

**Glossary**

- **Line Chart**: A graph that connects data points with lines, often used to show trends over time.
- **Pie Chart**: A circular chart divided into slices to represent proportions of a whole.
- **Box Plot**: A plot showing data distribution based on the minimum, first quartile, median, third quartile, and maximum.
- **Scatter Plot**: A graph displaying the relationship between two continuous variables using dots.
- **3D Plot**: A graph that visualizes data involving three continuous variables in three dimensions.
- **plot3D Package**: An R package for creating 3D plots like scatter, surface, and contour plots.
- **rgl Package**: An R package for interactive 3D plots, allowing rotation and zoom.
- **Saving Graphs**: Exporting a plot from R to a file format like PNG or PDF.
- **ggsave()**: A `ggplot2` function for saving plots with customizable format and size.
- **png(), jpeg(), tiff(), pdf()**: R functions for saving plots in different file formats.
- **dev.copy() and dev.print()**: R functions for copying or printing the current plot to a file.

# Exercise

**Exercise 1 – Multiple choice questions**
**1.** Which R package is primarily used for creating advanced, customizable graphs?
**a.** plot3D
**b.** rgl
**c.** ggplot2
**d.** base

**2.** In ggplot2, which component maps data variables to visual attributes like position and color?
**a.** Geometries (geom)
**b.** Layers
**c.** Themes
**d.** Aesthetics (aes)

**Exercise 2 – Fill in the blanks**
1. A ________ is a chart that uses bars to represent categorical data, with bar length proportional to value.
2. The ________ package in R is used for creating 3D plots like scatter, surface, and contour plots.

**Exercise 3 – True or False**
1. A density plot is similar to a histogram but uses a smoothed curve to represent the probability density of data.
2. ggplot2 is used for creating 3D plots in R.

**Exercise 4 – Short question answers**
1. Explain the difference between a histogram and a density plot.
2. What are the primary uses of the ggsave() function in R?

**Exercise 5 – Long question answers**
1. Discuss the role of layers in ggplot2 and how they contribute to building complex visualizations. Provide an example.
2. Describe the process of creating and customizing a 3D plot in R using the plot3D and rgl packages.

# Answers

**Exercise 1** – 1. c) 2. d)
**Exercise 2** – 1. bar plot 2. Plot3D
**Exercise 3** – 1. True 2. False

**Online Resources**

**Project Video**
**Link** : https://forms.gle/mDmNaKXkvW4ABX2CA
**QR Code**

**Practice Paper**

**Link**: https://www.youtube.com/playlist?list=PLzlh_31VWEFpceOF_fpymu83Q-up8dYvO
**QR Code**

**YouTube Video Playlist Link**
**Link**
https://www.youtube.com/playlist?list=PLzlh_31VWEFpceOF_fpymu83Q-up8dYvO
**QR Code**

**Test Paper**

**Chapter-11**
**Graphs**

**Time Duration: 40 Minutes** **Maximum Marks: 25**

**General Instructions:**
1. The question paper consists of 12 questions and is divided into four sections, A, B, C and D.
2. All questions are compulsory.
3. Section A comprises MCQs, Fill in the blanks and True or False carrying one marks each.
4. Section B comprises VSAQs(very short answers questions) carrying two marks each.
5. Section C comprises SAQs(short questions) carrying four marks each.
6. Section D comprises long questions carrying five marks each.

## SECTION-A

**I. Multiple choice questions:** **(1*2=2)**

1. Which type of plot is ideal for visualizing the distribution of data into bins?
a. Scatter Plot
b. Histogram
c. Line Chart
d. Box Plot

2. Which function is used in R to save a plot in a PNG format?
a. ggsave()
b. dev.print()
c. plot3D()
d. png()

**II. Fill in the blanks:** **(1*2=2)**

1. A ________ plot shows data distribution based on the minimum, first quartile, median, third quartile, and maximum.
2. In ggplot2, ________ modify non-data elements like text and backgrounds in a plot.

**III. True or False:** **(1*2=2)**

1. A scatter plot displays the relationship between two continuous variables using bars.
2. The aes() function in ggplot2 is used to save plots in various file formats.

## SECTION-B

**IV. Very Short answers type questions-I** **(2*3=6)**

1. What is the purpose of a pie chart?
2. Name the ggplot2 component used to map data variables to visual attributes.
3. Which R package is used for creating interactive 3D plots?

## SECTION-C

**V. Short answers type questions-II** **(4*2=8)**

1. Describe the key features of a box plot.
2. How do themes in ggplot2 enhance data visualization?

## SECTION-D

**VI. Long answers type questions** **(5*1=5)**

1. Explain the significance of data visualization in data analysis and how ggplot2 facilitates this in R. Include examples of different types of plots and their applications.

# Chapter 12: Data Interfaces

**In this chapter you will learn about**
- CSV File
- Excel File
- Binary File
- JSON File
- XML File
- Database

**Data Interfaces**
Data Interfaces refer to the various methods and tools available in R for reading, writing, and interacting with different types of data storage formats and systems. These interfaces allow users to import data from external sources into R for analysis, as well as export processed data from R to be used in other applications or stored for future use. R provides a rich ecosystem of packages and functions to handle a wide variety of data formats, making it highly versatile for data science and statistical computing.

**12.1 CSV File in Detail**
CSV (Comma-Separated Values) is a widely used format for storing tabular data, where each line in the file corresponds to a row of the table, and the values within each row are separated by commas. CSV files are simple, easy to read, and compatible across various applications and platforms, making them a popular choice for data exchange and storage.

**12.1.1 Structure of a CSV File:** A CSV file typically looks like this:

| | A | B | C |
|---|---|---|---|
| 1 | Name | Age | City |
| 2 | John Doe | 29 | New York |
| 3 | Jane Smith | 34 | Los Angeles |
| 4 | Emily Jones | 42 | Chicago |

- **Header Row:** The first row often contains the column names (Name, Age, City).
- **Data Rows:** Each subsequent row contains the actual data, with each value separated by a comma.

**12.1.2 Handling CSV Files in R:** R provides robust functionality for reading from and writing to CSV files through the read.csv() and write.csv() functions.

- **Reading CSV Files:** To read data from a CSV file into R, you can use the read.csv() function. This function reads the contents of a CSV file and loads it into a DataFrame, which is a table-like structure in R suitable for data manipulation.

```
# Reading a CSV file
data <- read.csv("path/to/your/file.csv")

# Display the first few rows of the data
head(data)
```

**Output:**

```
     Name      Age    City
1  John Doe    29   New York
2  Jane Smith  34   Los Angeles
3  Emily Jones 42   Chicago
```

- Parameters:
- **file:** Path to the CSV file.
- **header:** Logical value indicating whether the first row contains column names (TRUE by default).
- **sep:** The delimiter used in the file (, by default for CSV).
- **stringsAsFactors:** If TRUE, character vectors are converted to factors (default is TRUE in older versions of R, but FALSE in recent versions).

**12.1.3 Handling Missing Values:**

```
data <- read.csv("path/to/your/file.csv", na.strings = c("", "NA"))
```

Here, empty strings and "NA" are treated as missing values.

**12.1.4 Writing to CSV Files:** To export data from R to a CSV file, the write.csv() function is used. This function writes the contents of a DataFrame to a CSV file, allowing you to save the results of your analysis.

```
# Writing a DataFrame to a CSV file
write.csv(data, "path/to/save/your/file.csv", row.names = FALSE)
```

- Parameters:
- **x:** The DataFrame to write.
- **file:** Path where the CSV file will be saved.
- **row.names:** Logical value indicating whether to write row names to the file (FALSE by default).

**12.1.5 Customizing the CSV Reading/Writing Process:** R allows you to customize how you read from and write to CSV files by adjusting the parameters in read.csv() and write.csv().

- **Custom Delimiter:** If your data uses a different delimiter (e.g., a semicolon ;), you can specify it using the sep parameter.

```
data <- read.csv("path/to/your/file.csv", sep = ";")
```

- **Handling Large Files:** For very large files, you may prefer to use data.table::fread() from the data.table package, which is faster and more memory-efficient than read.csv().

```
library(data.table)
data <- fread("path/to/your/large_file.csv")
```

**12.1.6 Practical Considerations:** Encoding: Ensure that the correct file encoding is specified, especially if the CSV file contains non-ASCII characters. Use the fileEncoding parameter if necessary.

```
data <- read.csv("path/to/your/file.csv", fileEncoding = "UTF-8")
```

- **Dealing with Quotes:** CSV files may contain quoted text, especially if the data contains commas. The quote parameter in write.csv() and read.csv() helps manage this.

```
write.csv(data, "path/to/save/your/file.csv", quote = TRUE)
```

**12.1.6 Additional CSV Handling Packages:** While read.csv() and write.csv() are the base functions, several packages in R provide enhanced functionality for working with CSV files:

- **readr Package:** Offers functions like read_csv() and write_csv() that are faster and provide more control over how data is read and written.

```
library(readr)
```

```
data <- read_csv("path/to/your/file.csv")
```

**Output:**

```
New names:
• `` -> `...1`
Rows: 3 Columns: 4
── Column specification ────
Delimiter: ","
chr (2): Name, City
dbl (2): ...1, Age

i Use `spec()` to retrieve the full column specification for this data.
i Specify the column types or set `show_col_types = FALSE` to quiet this message.
```

- **data.table Package:** Provides fread() and fwrite() for fast reading and writing of CSV files, especially useful for large datasets.

```
library(data.table)
data <- fread("path/to/your/large_file.csv")
```

### 12.2 Excel File in R (Summary)

Excel files are widely used for data storage in a tabular format. R provides several packages to handle Excel files efficiently:

#### 12.2.1 Reading Excel Files

```
install.packages("readxl")
library(readxl)
data <- read_excel("path/to/file.xlsx", sheet = "Sheet1")
```

- **Features:** Handles both .xls and .xlsx formats, reads specific sheets, ranges, and allows column type specification.

#### 12.2.2 Writing Excel Files

```
install.packages("writexl")
library(writexl)
write_xlsx(data, "path/to/save/file.xlsx")
```

- **Features:** Simple writing of data to Excel files.

#### 12.2.3 Advanced Operations

```
install.packages("openxlsx")
library(openxlsx)
wb <- createWorkbook()
addWorksheet(wb, "Sheet1")
writeData(wb, "Sheet1", data)
saveWorkbook(wb, "path/to/save/file.xlsx", overwrite = TRUE)
```

- **Features:** Supports multiple sheets, custom formatting, and charts.

**Best Practices:** Use readxl for reading, writexl for simple writing, and openxlsx for advanced tasks like formatting and charts.

### 12.3 Binary Files

Binary files store data in a format that is optimized for both storage and retrieval, but is not human-readable. Instead of storing data as plain text, which is how CSV or text files do, binary files store data in the form of bytes. This makes binary files more efficient in terms of both file size and processing speed, especially for large datasets.

**Key Concepts of Binary Files**
- **Efficiency:** Binary files take up less space and can be read and written faster than text files because they are stored in a compressed, non-readable format.
- **Non-Readable:** Unlike text files, binary files cannot be easily read by humans. They require specific programs or functions to decode and interpret the data.
- **Structure:** Binary files often have a specific structure defined by the program that reads or writes them. This structure must be known and followed for correct data retrieval.

**Working with Binary Files in R**
R provides several functions to read and write binary data, depending on the level of control you need. Here are the main methods to handle binary files in R:

**12.3.1 Saving and Loading R Objects as Binary Files:** The simplest way to save R objects (like data frames, lists, or models) in a binary format is using the save() and load() functions. These functions save and restore the entire workspace or individual objects.

- Saving R Objects:

```
save(object1, object2, file = "mydata.RData")
```

This command saves the objects object1 and object2 into a binary file named "mydata.RData".
- Loading R Objects:

```
save(object1, object2, file = "mydata.RData")
```

This command restores the objects stored in "mydata.RData" back into the R environment.

**12.3.2 Reading and Writing Raw Binary Data:** For more control over the binary data, you can use the readBin() and writeBin() functions. These functions are used when you need to read or write raw binary data, such as when working with custom binary formats.

- Writing Binary Data:

```
con <- file("mybinaryfile.bin", "wb")

# Write binary data to the file
writeBin(c(1, 2, 3, 4, 5), con)

# Close the connection
close(con)
```

This code writes a sequence of numbers as binary data to a file named "mybinaryfile.bin".

- Reading Binary Data:

```
con <- file("mybinaryfile.bin", "rb")

# Read binary data from the file
data <- readBin(con, what = "integer", n = 5)
close(con)

# View the data
print(data)
```

This code reads five integers from the binary file "mybinaryfile.bin" into the variable data.

- **Specifying Data Types:** The what argument in readBin() specifies the type of data you are reading (e.g., "integer", "numeric", "character"). The n argument specifies the number of elements to read.

**12.3.3 Handling Complex Data Structures:** When working with more complex data structures, such as matrices or custom data formats, binary files can be more challenging. You'll need to carefully manage how the data is written and read, often involving manual specification of sizes, offsets, and data types.

- Writing and Reading a Matrix:

```
mat <- matrix(1:9, nrow = 3, ncol = 3)
con <- file("matrix.bin", "wb")
writeBin(as.numeric(mat), con)
close(con)

con <- file("matrix.bin", "rb")
mat_read <- matrix(readBin(con, what = "numeric", n = 9), nrow = 3, ncol = 3)
close(con)

print(mat_read)
```

This code writes a 3x3 matrix to a binary file and then reads it back, reconstructing the matrix in R.

**Use Cases of Binary Files**
- **Storing Large Data:** When working with large datasets, binary files are more space-efficient and faster to process than text formats.
- **Serialization:** Saving R objects like models, data frames, or lists in binary format for later use.
- **Custom Binary Formats:** Interfacing with systems or devices that require data in specific binary formats.

**12.4 JSON File**
JSON (JavaScript Object Notation) is a lightweight data-interchange format that is easy for humans to read and write and easy for machines to parse and generate. JSON is language-independent and is often used to transmit data between a server and web application, as well as for data storage in various applications. JSON files is facilitated by the jsonlite package, which provides a comprehensive set of tools for converting between R objects and JSON format.

**Key Features of JSON:**
- **Human-readable format:** JSON uses text that is easily readable by humans.
- **Structured data:** JSON structures data in key-value pairs, similar to dictionaries in Python or lists in R.
- **Hierarchical:** JSON supports nested data, which allows complex data structures like lists of lists, making it versatile for various data storage needs.

**Working with JSON in R**
**12.4.1 Installing the jsonlite Package:** To work with JSON files in R, you first need to install the jsonlite package if it's not already installed:

```
install.packages("jsonlite")
```

**12.4.2 Reading JSON Files:** JSON data can be read into R using the fromJSON() function provided by the jsonlite package. The function converts JSON data into R data structures such as lists or data frames.

```
install.packages("jsonlite")
```

- Reading a simple JSON file

```
library(jsonlite)

# Reading JSON from a file
data <- fromJSON("path/to/your/file.json")

# Viewing the structure of the imported data
str(data)
```

- Reading JSON from a URL

```
json_data <- fromJSON("https://api.example.com/data.json")
print(json_data)
```

**12.4.3 Writing JSON Files:** R data structures can be converted to JSON format using the toJSON() function and then written to a file or used directly in web applications.

```
# Creating a simple list in R
data <- list(name = "John", age = 30, occupation = "Data Scientist")

# Converting the R object to JSON
json_data <- toJSON(data, pretty = TRUE)

# Writing JSON to a file
write(json_data, file = "path/to/save/your/file.json")
```

The pretty = TRUE option formats the JSON output with indentation and line breaks, making it more human-readable.

**12.4.4 Handling Complex JSON Structures:** JSON can represent complex data structures, such as nested lists and arrays. The fromJSON() function in R will automatically detect and convert these structures into equivalent R objects.

```
# Nested JSON structure
json_content <- '{
  "employee": {
    "name": "Jane",
    "age": 29,
    "skills": ["R", "Python", "SQL"],
    "address": {
      "street": "123 Main St",
      "city": "Anytown",
      "state": "CA"
    }
  }
}'

# Convert JSON string to R object
data <- fromJSON(json_content)

# Accessing nested data
print(data$employee$name)  # "Jane"
print(data$employee$address$city)  # "Anytown"
```

**12.4.5 Converting Data Frames to JSON:** You can also convert an R data frame to JSON format using toJSON(). This is particularly useful when you need to export data from R to be used in web applications or APIs.

- Converting a data frame to JSON

```
# Creating a sample data frame
df <- data.frame(
  name = c("Alice", "Bob", "Charlie"),
  age = c(25, 30, 35),
  occupation = c("Analyst", "Developer", "Manager")
)

# Convert the data frame to JSON
json_data <- toJSON(df, pretty = TRUE)
```

```
# Write JSON to a file
write(json_data, file = "path/to/save/your/data.json")
```

**12.4.6 Validating and Parsing JSON Data:** JSON data can sometimes contain errors or be malformed. The validate() function in the jsonlite package helps in checking if a JSON string is valid.

```
valid <- validate('{"name": "John", "age": 30}')
print(valid)  # TRUE

invalid <- validate('{"name": "John", "age": }')
print(invalid)  # FALSE with error message
```

**12.4.7 Converting JSON to Other Formats:** Once JSON data is loaded into R, you can manipulate it like any other R object, converting it to data frames, lists, or other structures for further analysis or visualization.

```
json_content <- '[
  {"name": "Alice", "age": 25},
  {"name": "Bob", "age": 30}
]'

data <- fromJSON(json_content)
df <- as.data.frame(data)
print(df)
```

**12.5 XML File in R**

XML (eXtensible Markup Language) is a markup language that defines a set of rules for encoding documents in a format that is both human-readable and machine-readable. XML is commonly used to represent complex data structures, such as configuration files, data exchange formats in web services, and hierarchical data storage.

**Key Concepts in XML**

- **Elements:** Basic building blocks of an XML document. Each element is defined by a start tag <tag> and an end tag </tag>. Elements can contain text, other elements (nested elements), or be empty.
- **Attributes:** Additional information about elements provided in the start tag. For example, <element attribute="value">.
- **Hierarchy:** XML data is structured hierarchically, with ncsted elements representing the relationships between different pieces of data.

**Working with XML in R**

**12.5.1 Reading XML Files:** The xml2 package in R provides the read_xml() function to read XML files into an R object, which you can then manipulate.

```
install.packages("xml2")
library(xml2)
xml_data <- read_xml("path/to/your/file.xml")
```

**12.5.2 Navigating and Extracting Data:** Once the XML file is loaded, you can navigate through its structure and extract the data you need.

- Extracting elements:

```
specific_elements <- xml_find_all(xml_data, "//tagname")
```

- Extracting text content:

```
specific_elements <- xml_find_all(xml_data, "//tagname")
```

- Extracting attributes:

```
attributes <- xml_attr(specific_elements, "attribute_name")
```

**12.5.3 Modifying XML Data:** You can modify the XML data in R before writing it back to an XML file.

- Adding a new element:

```
new_element <- xml_add_child(xml_data, "newtag", "content")
```

- Modifying an existing element:

```
xml_set_text(specific_elements, "new content")
```

- Changing an attribute value:

```
xml_set_attr(specific_elements,"attribute_name", "new_value")
```

**12.5.4 Writing to an XML File:** After processing or modifying the XML data, you can write it back to an XML file using the write_xml() function.

- Writing the XML data to a file:

```
xml_set_attr(specific_elements,"attribute_name", "new_value")
```

**12.6 Databases in R**

Databases are structured collections of data that are managed using a database management system (DBMS). They are commonly used to store large amounts of data that need to be accessed, managed, and updated efficiently. Databases can range from small, single-user databases like SQLite to large, enterprise-level systems like MySQL, PostgreSQL, SQL Server, or Oracle.

**12.6.1 Connecting to a Database**: To interact with a database in R, you first need to establish a connection using the dbConnect() function from the DBI package. The specific driver (e.g., RSQLite, RMySQL, RPostgres) will depend on the type of database you're connecting to.

**- Connecting to a SQLite Database**

```
library(DBI)
con <- dbConnect(RSQLite::SQLite(), "path/to/your/database.sqlite")
```

**- Connecting to a MySQL Database**

```
library(DBI)
con <- dbConnect(RMySQL::MySQL(),
                 dbname = "your_database_name",
                 host = "your_host",
                 port = 3306,
                 user = "your_username",
                 password = "your_password")
```

**12.6.2 Querying Data:** Once connected, you can query data from the database using SQL queries with the `dbGetQuery()` function.

**- Querying Data**

```
data <- dbGetQuery(con, "SELECT * FROM your_table")
```

**12.6.3 Writing Data to a Database**: You can also write data from an R DataFrame to a database table using the `dbWriteTable()` function.

**- Writing Data**

```
dbWriteTable(con, "your_table", data)
```

**Updating and Deleting Data**: To update or delete data, you can use the dbExecute() function, which allows you to execute SQL commands that modify the database.

**- Updating Data**

```
dbExecute(con, "UPDATE your_table SET column1 = 'new_value' WHERE condition")
```

**- Deleting Data**

```
dbExecute(con, "DELETE FROM your_table WHERE condition")
```

**Disconnecting from a Database**: After completing your database operations, it's important to disconnect from the database using the dbDisconnect() function to free up resources.

**- Disconnecting**

```
dbDisconnect(con)
```

**12.6.4 Advanced Database Operations**

**- Transactions:** R supports database transactions, allowing you to perform a series of operations as a single unit of work. This ensures data integrity and consistency.

```
dbBegin(con)
dbExecute(con, "SQL command")
dbCommit(con)  # or dbRollback(con) to undo the transaction
```

**- Prepared Statements:** For efficient execution of repeated queries, you can use prepared statements.

```
stmt <- dbSendStatement(con, "INSERT INTO your_table (column1, column2) VALUES (?, ?)")
dbBind(stmt, list(value1, value2))
dbClearResult(stmt)
```

**- Batch Processing:** If you need to insert or update a large amount of data, batch processing techniques can be employed to improve performance.

**Summary**

- **CSV (Comma-Separated Values)**: A text format for storing tabular data, with values separated by commas.
- **Data Frame**: A table-like structure in R for storing and manipulating data.
- **Delimiter**: A character used to separate values in a text file (e.g., commas in CSV).
- **JSON (JavaScript Object Notation)**: A lightweight format for storing and transmitting structured data.
- **XML (eXtensible Markup Language)**: A markup language for encoding hierarchical data in a readable format.

**Glossary**

- **DBMS (Database Management System)**: Software that manages and organizes data in databases.
- **DBI (Database Interface)**: An R package for connecting and interacting with databases.
- **Binary File**: A file storing data in a non-readable format, optimized for storage and speed.
- **Transactions**: A series of database operations treated as a single, atomic unit.
- **Prepared Statements**: Precompiled SQL queries for efficient repeated execution.

**Exercise 1 – Multiple choice questions**

**1.** Which of the following is a lightweight format for storing and transmitting structured data?
**a.** CSV
**b.** XML
**c.** JSON
**d.** Binary File

**2.** What does the DBI package in R facilitate?
**a.** Creating visualizations

**b.** Connecting and interacting with databases
**c.** File compression
**d.** Data cleaning

**Exercise 2 – Fill in the blanks**
1. A ________ is a text format for storing tabular data, with values separated by commas.
2. The ________ package in R is used for connecting and interacting with databases.

**Exercise 3 – True or False**
1. JSON is a markup language used for encoding hierarchical data.
2. A Data Frame in R is used to store and manipulate data in a table-like structure.

**Exercise 4 – Short question answers**
1. Describe the role of a delimiter in a text file.
2. Explain the difference between JSON and XML.

**Exercise 5 – Long question answers**
1. Discuss the advantages of using binary files for data storage and retrieval. Include examples of when binary files are preferable over text formats.
2. Explain the significance of transactions in database operations. How do they contribute to data integrity and consistency?

## Answers

**Exercise 1** – 1. c) 2. b)
**Exercise 2** – 1. CSV 2. DBI
**Exercise 3** – 1. False 2. True

### Online Resources

**Practice Paper**
**Link:** https://forms.gle/aZkQ3jPdyot2EtYX9
**QR Code**

**Project Video**
**Link:** https://www.youtube.com/playlist?list=PLzlh_31VWEFqHzLYhCQhOb0uNooMGixiL
**QR Code**

**YouTube Video Playlist Link**
**Link:** https://www.youtube.com/playlist?list=PLzlh_31VWEFqHzLYhCQhOb0uNooMGixiL
**QR Code**

**Test Paper**
**Chapter-12**
**Data Interfaces**

**Time Duration: 40 Minutes** **Maximum Marks: 25**

**General Instructions:**
1. The question paper consists of 12 questions and is divided into four sections, A, B, C and D.
2. All questions are compulsory.
3. Section A comprises MCQs, Fill in the blanks and True or False carrying one marks each.
4. Section B comprises VSAQs(very short answers questions) carrying two marks each.
5. Section C comprises SAQs(short questions) carrying four marks each.
6. Section D comprises long questions carrying five marks each.

## SECTION-A

**I. Multiple choice questions:** **(1*2=2)**
1. Which file format is optimized for storage and speed, storing data in a non-readable format?
a. CSV
b. JSON
c. Binary File
d. XML

2. What is the main function of a DBMS (Database Management System)?
a. Generating reports
b. Managing and organizing data in databases
c. Creating charts
d. Editing text files

**II. Fill in the blanks:** **(1*2=2)**
1. A ________ is a character used to separate values in a text file, such as commas in CSV files.
2. ________ is a markup language used for encoding hierarchical data in a readable format

**III. True or False:** **(1*2=2)**
1. CSV files store data in a non-readable binary format optimized for speed.
2. XML is used for storing and transmitting structured data.

## SECTION-B

**IV. Very Short answers type questions-I** **(2*3=6)**
1. What is the primary purpose of a Database Management System (DBMS)?
2. Name the file format that uses commas to separate values in a table.
3. What is a Data Frame in R?

## SECTION-C

**V. Short answers type questions-II** **(4*2=8)**
1. What are prepared statements, and why are they useful in SQL?
2. How does the DBI package assist in working with databases in R?

## SECTION-D

**VI. Long answers type questions** **(5*1=5)**

1. Compare and contrast JSON, CSV, and XML formats in terms of structure, readability, and common use cases. Provide examples of scenarios where each format would be most appropriate.

## ADDITIONAL RESOURCES

**R Programming Insights Videos Playlist-**

**Link:** https://www.youtube.com/playlist?list=PLzlh_31VWEFriD13GDFJ4SSzKq5qQALKH

**QR Code:**

**R Programming Insights Project Videos Playlist-**

**Link:** https://www.youtube.com/playlist?list=PLzlh_31VWEFqOi3GZBTWVvobZM95F29hp

**QR Code:**

## In this book

Welcome to "R Programming Insights: From" your definitive guide to mastering R programming. This book offers a balanced mix of foundational concepts and advanced techniques, crafted to meet the needs of both beginners and experienced programmers. Whether you're a student, data scientist, or analyst, you'll discover invaluable tools and resources to sharpen your skills and achieve your data analysis goals. Dive in and unlock the potential of R to transform data into insights that drive informed decisions.

## YouTube Videos Playlists for all Chapters

**CHAPTER 1**
**Link:** https://www.youtube.com/playlist?list=PLzlh_31VWEFoXTJqrHt_nW5s247CwygsR
**QR Code**

**CHAPTER 2**

**Link:** https://www.youtube.com/playlist?list=PLzlh_31VWEFowmPaYw2tdGdroPuQKKxC8
**QR Code:**

**CHAPTER 3**
**Link:** https://www.youtube.com/playlist?list=PLzlh_31VWEFqQ_cS64zGtSbhdGI0d7sUv
**QR Code**

**CHAPTER 4**
**Link:** https://www.youtube.com/playlist?list=PLzlh_31VWEFp3OchKlozdoioCmNZ2TcBp
**QR Code**

**CHAPTER 5**
**Link:** https://www.youtube.com/playlist?list=PLzlh_31VWEFrAujKi1tG2DEqZBVWihQvQ
**QR Code**

**CHAPTER 6**
**Link:** https://www.youtube.com/playlist?list=PLzlh_31VWEFrQ6O5XafGpfNYykxPgAUld
**QR Code**

**CHAPTER 7**
**Link:** https://www.youtube.com/playlist?list=PLzlh_31VWEFrAujKi1tG2DEqZBVWihQvQ
**QR Code**

**CHAPTER 8**
**Link:** https://www.youtube.com/playlist?list=PLzlh_31VWEFrQ6O5XafGpfNYykxPgAUld
**QR Code**

**CHAPTER 9**
**Link:** https://www.youtube.com/playlist?list=PLzlh_31VWEFqovzf2UzHSiL3b6U2ygyuw
**QR Code**

**CHAPTER 10**
**Link:** https://www.youtube.com/playlist?list=PLzlh_31VWEFqz3IgIy54-ZbzbOcep_Fgv
**QR code**

**CHAPTER 11**
**Link:** https://www.youtube.com/playlist?list=PLzlh_31VWEFpceOF_fpymu83Q-up8dYvO
**QR Code**

**CHAPTER 12**
**Link** https://www.youtube.com/playlist?list=PLzlh_31VWEFqHzLYhCQhOb0uNooMGixiL
**QR Code**